S0-AQL-216

HOW TO SURVIVE BEING ALIVE

HOW TO SURVIVE BEING ALIVE

DONALD L. DUDLEY, M.D.
and ELTON WELKE

Doubleday & Company, Inc., Garden City, New York, 1977

Acknowledgment is gratefully extended to the following for permission to reprint from their works:

"Old Friends" © 1968 Paul Simon. Used by permission.

"Hello in There" by John Prine © 1971 Cotillion Music Inc. and Sour Grapes Music. All Rights Reserved. Used by permission.

"Give Your Heart to the Hawks" © 1973 Winfred Blevins, by permission of Nash Publishing Corporation.

ISBN: 0-385-12107-5
Library of Congress Catalog Card Number: 76-50763

Printed in the United States of America
First Edition

to Thomas H. Holmes, M.D.,
teacher and scholar

CONTENTS

1 SOME NEW CONCEPTS AND SOME OLD FANTASIES 1
2 STRESS IS? 9
3 THE MIND-BODY NONSENSE 21
4 PSYCHOBIOLOGIC SHORT CIRCUITS 35
5 THE IMPACT OF LIFE CHANGE 45
6 COPING BEHAVIORS 61
7 THE COLTER COASTER 75
8 THE UPS AND DOWNS OF DISEASE 89
9 THE ART OF BEING SUCCESSFULLY SICK 111
10 WHEN YOUR BOSS GIVES YOU A HEADACHE 127
11 SURVIVAL IN THE REAL WORLD 141
EPILOGUE—A CHECKLIST FOR SURVIVAL 161
BIBLIOGRAPHY 165

To be, or not to be: that is the question:
Whether 'tis nobler in the mind to suffer
The slings and arrows of outrageous fortune,
Or to take arms against a sea of troubles,
And by opposing end them?

—Hamlet, Prince of Denmark

There are many things more important
than comfort and a few even more important
than health. But a man should appreciate
what his actions and goals are costing him.

—Harold G. Wolff, M.D.

HOW TO SURVIVE BEING ALIVE

CHAPTER 1

SOME NEW CONCEPTS AND SOME OLD FANTASIES

For centuries, patients and physicians alike have attributed accidents to bad luck or bad timing, carelessness, acts of God, fickleness of weather, or unbanked turns in the road. Similarly, most of today's medical scientists, secure with the past hundred years' discoveries of bacteria, biochemical defects, viruses, and genetic inheritance, link diseases to specific identifiable causes—germs, malfunctions in body chemistry, environmental factors, bad water or bad parents. Thus, you have the flu because you "caught a virus." If you develop diabetes, it's because your pancreas "stopped doing its job properly." You "inherited" your weak heart from your father or mother. You were "born" with your chronic hay fever. And you "lost control" of your car because the road was slippery. These are time-honored and comfortable myths for both patients and doctors. They provide something pragmatic to work with. Broken bones are set, medicines are prescribed, surgical procedures are performed with skilled and practiced hands.

Yet consider this startling fact: medical records indicate *70 per cent of those medical treatments and surgical procedures are administered to only 30 per cent of us*. To be sure, most of us are exposed to the same hazards of viruses, bad roads, and stomach acids. But only about one in three of us actually goes to bed with the flu, skids off the highway, or develops a stomach ulcer when such threats present themselves. The other two, even though subject to the same risks, stay healthy.

If that confounds you, ponder still another outrageous fact: within any large sampling of patients suffering from related *chronic disease* (a group of heart patients, for instance), a *predictable* number of them will get well; a *predictable* number will die; and a *predictable* number will stay the same, neither improving nor deteriorating in health, *regardless of the nature or quality of medical treatment*. In this context, the witch doctor's patients are no different from those of the skilled heart specialist. The quack and the expert can expect about the same rates of recovery and mortality among certain of their patients.[1]

Why do some workers in an office catch colds when "the bug" is going around, while others do not? All of them are exposed to the same viruses. More curious still, why do some workers catch colds every winter, while others do not? And why do some workers catch not only the seasonal colds each year, but also the flu, as well as suffer sinus headaches, ailments resulting from accidents, and chronic skin problems? Meanwhile, others in the same office always glow with "good health." And why among all of us do some 10 to 20 per cent never get sick? *Never!*

At long last, answers to these puzzles are surfacing.

Let's look at two hypothetical, yet typical, case histories that provide some insight into what makes people sick.

First is Martha, married six years, employed as a copywriter for a major advertising agency in New York. She likes her work, and at leisure she delights in decorating the apartment she and her husband rent. She has a discerning eye for contemporary art and funky antiques.

[1] If you are *acutely ill*, however, the medical expert is insurance you will survive. In the hands of a quack you probably will not.

As fortune will have it, her husband's affair with his secretary leads to a divorce. Understandably, Martha is disoriented and saddened by the whole distasteful episode. She decides to "start a fresh life, to straighten her act out, to wipe the slate clean."

A few weeks after the divorce is final, Martha quits her job at the agency, sublets the apartment, moves to San Francisco, rents a flat on Telegraph Hill, finds a job as an editorial assistant with a small local magazine, buys a new sports car, and, before driving it even 200 miles, precipitates a head-on collision on the Golden Gate Bridge. Her injuries put Martha in a hospital for two months.

The second case is Hal, married thirty-eight years, father of a grown daughter with a family of her own. Hal lives in Seattle, in a house he constructed himself some twenty years ago. He retired as an engineer at Boeing Corporation last year, and now spends his time growing camellias and fishing for salmon.

Suddenly, without advance warning, Hal's wife dies of a heart attack. He is bereaved, near despair. It's only with the help of his minister and his daughter, who flies up from San Diego, that he makes it through the crisis without having a nervous collapse.

"Sell the house and come live with us," pleads his daughter.

So he does. Within weeks the house is sold, and Hal moves to San Diego. A few days after settling in with his daughter, son-in-law, and grandchildren, he suffers a fatal stroke.

Applying research pioneered by psychophysiologist Thomas H. Holmes, our Martha and Hal were respectively injured and killed by stresses resulting from the accumulative effects of "life changes."

In a scientific bombshell, a virtual moonshot in psychiatry, Dr. Holmes and Dr. Richard H. Rahe formally introduced the Social Readjustment Rating Scale to science in 1967. The Social Readjustment Rating Scale consists of forty-three "life change" events with a point value assigned to each event. Through extensive research, Holmes, Rahe, and their colleagues have discovered that should you accumulate 150 points on the Social Readjustment Rating Scale within a period of two years, there is a 33 per cent probability for you to contract an illness or suffer an accident. When 300 points are accumulated, the probability soars to 66 per cent. At 450 points the probability is almost certain–in the 90 per cent range.

If Martha had only experienced her divorce (73 points on Dr. Holmes' scale) and had made no other major life changes for, say, eighteen months, she would probably have remained healthy. Instead, she changed to a different line of work (36 points on the Social Readjustment Rating Scale), changed her living conditions (25 points), changed her personal habits (24 points), changed residence (20 points), and obtained a loan of under $10,000 (17 points) for the new car. Martha's total score was at least 195 when she drifted over that center line.

We can guess her accumulative score was even higher. She likely had trouble sleeping through all those moves and disruptions (16 points). Her eating habits may well have changed (15 points). Her social activities certainly changed (18 points).

Had Martha kept her job in New York after the divorce, stayed in the apartment, and continued to collect her art, it's improbable she would have suffered such a serious accident.

Hal was dangerously close to trouble before he ever left Seattle. His retirement (one year before his wife died) netted him 45 points. His wife's sudden death added a devastating 100 points. The sale of his house brought Hal $96,000 in cash, a financial windfall. But it also added 38 points by significantly changing his financial state. The move, of course, changed his living conditions (25 points), residence (20 points), and personal habits (24 points). Even without counting changes in church activities (19 points), changes in social activities (18 points), changes in sleeping habits (16 points), or eating habits (15 points), Hal accumulated 15 points because of the change in frequency of family get-togethers.

At absolute minimum, Hal had 267 points on the Social Readjustment Rating Scale. A Christmas would have added 12 points, a speeding ticket 11 points.

Hal was in mortally serious trouble the day his daughter convinced him to sell the house and move south. Neither of them realized it—they both thought they were doing the best thing for Hal's comfort and peace of mind.

If Hal had understood how stresses brought on by life changes can influence one's susceptibility to illnesses and accidents, he could have saved himself from premature disaster.

No one can eliminate stress from day-to-day living—nor would it be desirable. The world's vanguard authority on stress, Hans Selye, likes to say that "stress is the spice of life." Without stress we'd be dead, points out Dr. Selye. Ironically, too much stress achieves the same end.

You can't avoid the stressors of living. Everyone is faced with unavoidable life changes such as the deaths of relatives, business turns (either up or down), changes in fortune, and changes in climate. We all must deal with serious travail now and then. But when such inescapable circumstances occur, you can enormously reduce your probabilities for subsequent sickness by minimizing other stressful life changes that are *under your control.*

Understanding how life changes, good and bad, can accumulate to make you sick is perhaps the most valuable gain in preventive medicine ever achieved. Yet it's just a beginning. Besides an ability now to predict your chances for becoming ill or having an accident, with amazing accuracy, researchers in the intricate science of psychophysiology have developed penetrating insights into links between attitudes and illnesses. It started with a visionary neurologist named Harold G. Wolff, whose landmark monograph *Stress and Disease* was originally published in 1953. On his foundations, current studies have examined how specific attitudes and points of view correlate with particular illnesses. The results provoke re-examination of some old ideas about diseases.

The skin rash eczema, for example, has been linked with feelings of frustration. Essential high blood pressure appears in those of us who feel we must be on guard, prepared to meet all possible threats, ready for anything. A backache indicates a desire to escape, to run away, "to get out of there." Even heartburn has been examined. It results, according to convincing study, "when you are getting what you want."

Acne, traditionally associated with adolescence, plagues adults and teen-agers alike when they feel nagged at, picked upon, when they "want to be left alone." Attitudes that describe a majority of adolescents, to be sure—and some adults, the ones who suffer "adult skin problems."

In our society we cling to the notion a distinction exists between "physical" diseases and "mental" diseases. Traditionally, the two are separated like church and state. In reality, there are as many physical problems associated with "mental" diseases as there are mental problems associated with "physical" diseases. Nevertheless, most of us continue to look at illnesses in ways dictated by fashion rather than facts. In our society you retain your status as a "good person" if you have a disease that is considered organic or physical. Thus stricken, you deserve "time out," sympathy, and financial compensation. But if you have a psychiatric disease you are seen as a weak person (a legacy of ancient Greek tradition) or a sinful person (Hebrew tradition), or as having "bad blood" or bad parents.[2]

The irony is that for most "mental" and "physical" illnesses the precipitating cause is the same—stress.

By fashion we have been taught that the causes of medical and surgical diseases are known, yet in reality very little was understood about disease until recently, and we still operate in a scientific twilight. For decades, we've worked with myths in

[2] In our culture you don't qualify as sick unless you fulfill certain illness criteria (regardless of whether or not you have a disease). The traditional primary sign of illnesses is a loss of productivity ("I can no longer lift that tool"). The traditional primary symptom of illness is a loss of comfort ("It hurts when I move it").

the healing sciences, inventing "scientific" explanations to cover our lack of knowledge about the causative factors in illness. This often angers and discourages patients when they learn that the miracles of modern medicine will not cure them. It also frustrates their doctors.

Happily, breakthroughs emerging from the field of psychophysiology are helping to illuminate not only the major causes of illness, but ways to avoid those causes. Most of this work has only been announced in the past decade, and some of it has not yet been formally introduced to medicine. In total, its significance to your health cannot be overstated.

Except for the relatively small number of nutritional diseases, a few directly inherited diseases, and certain infectious diseases, it is evident today that stress and our reactions to stress are the major causes of illness. Accumulative research so overwhelmingly and convincingly proves this, it's almost shocking the results haven't been more widely celebrated, both within the medical community and by the public at large.[3]

Each of us can incorporate this information into our lives in ways constructive to better health. It requires no difficult training, technical skill, or apparatus. It didn't originate in the hills of India, scrolls from ancient cultures, or Hollywood health spas. It is a product of some of the world's finest medical research laboratories and keenest scientific minds. It heralds a new medical era, a quantum leap forward in knowledge—knowledge that can help you maintain good and improved health . . . or save your life.

[3] Customarily there is about a twenty-year lag between medical research and subsequent popular acceptance or clinical application by doctors and patients alike.

CHAPTER 2

STRESS IS?

Life is a wearing-down process. A collision at sea can hurry the job along. So can snake bite, an earthquake, or an angry spouse. But what overtakes most of us is stress that is not so readily apparent.

Stress? Few words in our language suffer more from diverse and ambiguous usage. Within the scientific community, definitions of psychological and physiological stress range confusingly from the sources of stress (fear, pressure, tension, cold) to the results of stress (asthma attack, nervous breakdown, frostbite). Hans Selye himself, the father of much that comprises modern stress theory, has over the years readjusted his definitions of the term. Broadly speaking, physiologists currently define stress as *an adaptive response in which your body prepares, or adjusts, to a threatening situation.* Thus stress is not pressure or tension, hardship, chill waters, or cold winds. These are *stressors,* conditions that may precipitate stress. And stress is not frozen fingers, accidents, "jangled nerves," or irascibility, although these are common results of stress.

As most recently defined by Selye, in 1974, stress *is the nonspecific response of the body to any demand made upon it.*

As you sprint up a flight of stairs, your blood pressure increases, your heart pumps faster, and more blood flows to your legs. Otherwise you couldn't climb the stairs. When exposed to cold, the capillary blood vessels in your skin contract to diminish heat loss. These represent stress, your body's responses to demands, and if they strike you as more an aid than a hindrance to good health, you are absolutely right. They are reactions appropriate to your body's needs. Without such reactions you couldn't survive. Indeed, without such stress our species would not have evolved.

WHAT MADE COLTER RUN?

The year is 1809, midsummer, early dawn on a beaver creek only a few miles from where the Jefferson, Madison, and Gallatin rivers join to form the Missouri. John Colter, the "first mountain man," a veteran of Lewis and Clark's 1804–5 expedition to the Pacific, is tending traps with another mountain man named Potts. The sun isn't up yet, but Colter feels jumpy, ill at ease. The morning fog is thinning, and soon their canoe will be visible from shore. They paddle toward the next trap. As the canoe glides by, Colter retrieves the trap from icy waters, pulling a drowned beaver with it into the canoe. Quietly, with practiced motions, he resets the trap and places it back on the stream bottom. Potts is happy. They've had a good morning's take. But he knows better than to talk needlessly in Blackfoot country. For weeks Potts and Colter have been trapping nights and laying low days. This is, after all, Indian country in 1809. Dangerous.

It's almost full daylight now, but there are still a few traps to be checked.

Suddenly, the sound of hoofs or feet. Something?

"Indians," whispers Colter. "Let's cache in them bushes."

"Buffler," says Potts. "Buffler trompin' around."

The two men listen, drifting indecisively. Then there they are with numbing suddenness, several hundred Blackfeet on both sides of the creek. The Indians motion for them to paddle ashore. Women and children are poking their heads through the crowds of braves. Potts is frozen with fear. Colter paddles in, beaching the canoe. As Potts hesitantly climbs out of the canoe, an Indian snatches his rifle. Colter, a powerful man, grabs the rifle and hands it back to Potts.

"Show them you aren't afraid of them," Colter tells Potts.

"You're crazy," responds Potts. "They're going to kill us."

Potts leaps back into the canoe and shoves off. An arrow, striking Potts in the hip, ends the escape. Doubled over with pain, Potts raises his rifle muzzle and fires, killing one of the Indian braves. Retaliation is swift as dozens of arrows riddle Potts, now half submerged alongside the swamped boat. With cries of revenge, braves, squaws, and children drag Potts' body from the creek and begin hacking at it with hatchets and knives.

Turning to Colter, the frenzied Blackfeet rip his clothes from him, jabbing him with fingers and fists. A squaw menacingly approaches Colter with something bloody in her hand. Potts' genitals. Screaming, she hurls them into Colter's face. Forcing himself to keep his eyes open and to stand straight, Colter is pelted with bloody pieces of Potts' mutilated corpse. With blurred vision, Colter can see several elder braves and chiefs debating what to do with him, what manner of torture to inflict. A chief walks over to him and asks if he is a runner. Colter takes a long time to answer–something canny is called for.

"I am a slow runner. Yes, the other white men say that I am very swift. But they are wrong. I am slow."

The chief walks back to the council. There certainly is no chance for Colter to outrun five hundred angry Indians. Still, if they want to make a game of it, it beats being hacked to death. The chief returns and instructs Colter to walk past a large boulder some two hundred yards from the Indians; then to run for his life. As Colter walks toward the rock on his bare feet, he glances back to see the younger braves shedding blankets and leggings for the sprint. He walks slowly, very slowly, past the boulder, hoping to maximize his lead before pursuit begins. A chorus of whoops starts the race and Colter takes off.

He heads for the Jefferson River, some six miles distant. He knows his chances are nil, absolutely hopeless, but only by reaching a river is survival even a remote possibility. The Blackfoot are expert trackers on land. *Run.*

As far ahead as Colter can see the landscape is rolling plains. He does not look back. He concentrates on his legs and lungs. *Run.*

Low-growing prickly-pear spines lacerate his feet. His breathing is speeding, his throat dry and aching. He feels his bowels will let go. *Run.*

How close are they? He wills his legs to reach out farther and faster, leap after leap. He must look back. A quick glance tells him most of the Indians are falling behind. They are scattered over the plain. Only one is close, perhaps a hundred yards distant. My God, there's a chance. A chance! *Run.*

Colter is getting dizzy. He fights the waves of nausea, forcing himself to keep his eyes open. His breathing is in gasps now, his chest heaves like a bellows. He looks back again. The fastest-pursuing Indian is only twenty yards behind, and he is carrying a spear, an ugly, deadly weapon that Colter can imagine plunged into his back. He concentrates on moving his legs faster. *Run.*

Something is splashing on Colter's knees. He looks down to see the front of his body covered with blood. Blood! He tastes it salty on his lips. Blood is gushing from his nose. Oh God, has he slowed down? He can't keep this up. He can't keep running. Colter abruptly stops.

Turning and spreading his arms he screams in fear and outrage. Startled and near exhaustion himself, the pursuing Indian attempts to stop and hurl his spear at the same time. He stumbles, falls forward, and gouges his spear into the ground, snapping its shaft in half. Before the brave can recover, Colter grabs the spearhead and plunges it into the Blackfoot, killing him.

Colter's legs seem to fill with new energy. He takes off for the river, now less than a mile away. In the distance behind him he hears the outcries as the Blackfeet discover their dead comrade. Reaching the Jefferson, Colter dives in, swims downstream, and finds a big pile of driftwood to swim under, climb up into, and hide. The Blackfeet search the riverbanks for hours but do not locate his hiding place. The following morning, cold, naked, and bloody, he heads for Fort Lisa, covering the two hundred miles in eleven days, arriving at last, footsore and hungry . . . and alive!

FIGHT AND FLIGHT

Fight and flight responses are bodily changes that prepare you for an emergency or threat or a need for sudden increased physical exertion. From the moment John Colter heard those footsteps that morning back in 1809, his body reacted in ways that helped him survive the following ordeals. At the first hint of threat, his brain notified a host of body mechanisms to prepare for action. His adrenal glands began pumping adrenaline and other hormones into his system. His circulation speeded up. His lungs pumped more air. His blood pressure soared. Increased amounts of energy-rich sugar appeared in his blood. His blood clotting mechanisms were accelerated. His muscle function improved. New blood cells were released from storage. His eyesight and hearing became keener. Meanwhile, his digestive system went into temporary dormancy. Without these stress reactions John Colter would have never escaped the Blackfeet. His built-in fight and flight responses brought him through.

In extensive and classic experiments with cats in the decade following 1910, Walter B. Cannon, a physiologist at Harvard, found that pain, physical injuries, starvation, intense emotion, an inadequate air supply, and sudden encounters with dogs all produced the same physical reactions associated with fight and flight.

The psychological and physiological chain of events in fight and flight response is simple enough at first blush:

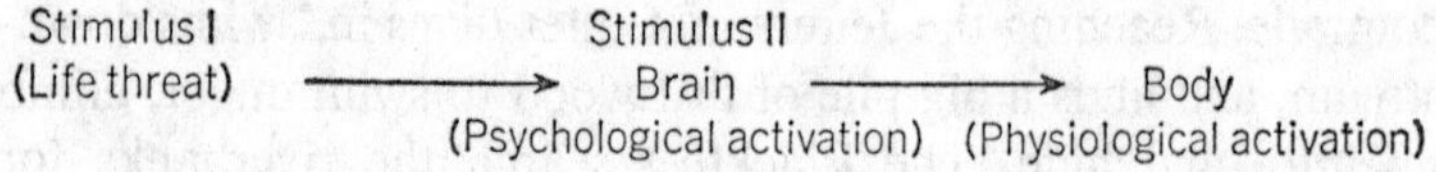

Stimulus I (Life threat) ⟶ Stimulus II Brain (Psychological activation) ⟶ Body (Physiological activation)

The threat is analyzed by the brain after receiving signals from the sensory organs (psychological activation) which in turn activates the body to deal with the threat in a way appropriate to survival (physiological activation).

How can such a stress reaction so obviously evolved over millions of years to help us survive also make us sick? One clue lies in the fact that merely thinking about a threatening situation can trigger fight and flight responses. A jet fighter pilot needn't have a missile tracking him to elicit emergency bodily changes. If the pilot happens to be the worrying sort, he'll spend a lot of time breathing hard and emptying his bowels in the hours before takeoff.

Most of us, of course, are not engaged in such overtly stressful activities as flying fighters, let alone the kind of day to day adventures John Colter faced.

Or are we?

Imagine you are John Colter, district sales manager for an international electronics corporation, and you've been examining the current sales reports trying to ferret out why your district's gross sales are up 8 per cent this year over last, but your net sales profits are down 14 per cent. Can business travel possibly have gotten that much out of hand? Then the call comes.

"This is Ms. Footsteps, secretary to Mr. Blackfoot, vice-president in charge of finance. He wonders if you could come to his office immediately and asks that you bring your current sales reports and budgets with you."

Run, John Colter, *run*.

Another aspect of the bodily changes associated with fight and flight responses is "feedback." Bodily and internal changes are themselves stimulators, and they may go on alerting the brain to continue fight and flight messages long after the actual threat has passed. For example, let's say your phone rings, you pick up the receiver and you hear a string of blunt sexual comments. You've got a kook on the line, an obscene caller. Your reaction is to calmly, or as calmly as you can considering how upset you really are, tell the jerk he's got a wrong number and hang up:

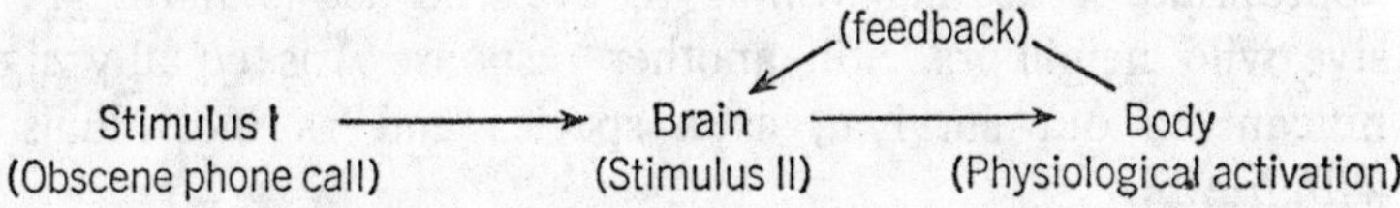

As you hang up, Stimulus #1 is gone, but your reaction to the call—anger, tensed muscles, increased blood pressure, and shortness of breath—may continue for some time, even though in fact these reactions are no longer required to help deal with the phone call:

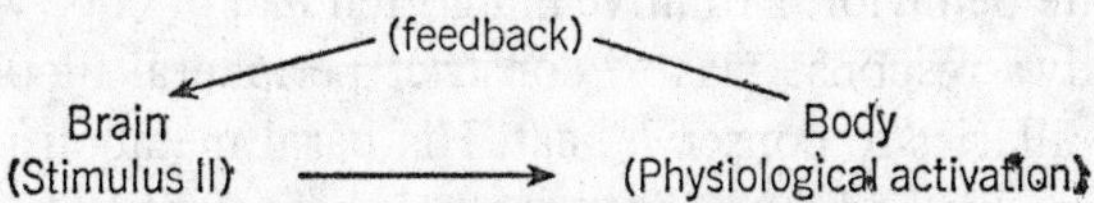

What's more, if the calls continue, the mere ringing of your phone may begin to serve as the Stimulus #1 to trigger the responses (remember Pavlov's dogs?). Anger at receiving the obscene phone call is an absolutely appropriate response, a healthy response. It assists you in dealing with the caller. However, the continued feedback responses after the call and the Pavlovian reaction subsequently to any ringing phone are inappropriate responses. They are not healthy or adaptive. What if the ringing of a friend's telephone elicits sudden anger? Or what if you get angry at a friend simply because he called you. If, in the extreme, your responses begin to keep you awake nights worrying, if they affect your appetite, or if they distract you from concentrating at work, then they may become destructive to your well being.

SOME STRESS RESPONSES ARE APPROPRIATE . . . OTHERS ARE NOT

Stress, an adaptive response to a threat, has been with us since our most ancient of ancestors first began ranging beyond the safety of crevices, caves, thick forests, or wherever they hid before overcoming their fears enough to venture out into sunlight. Over millions of years, fight and flight responses were appropriate to dealing with aggressive wild beasts and aggressive wild neighbors. Still another response was equally significant to our survival, as a species and as individuals—*withdrawal*.

When a saber-toothed tiger was stalking, retreat was appropriate behavior. When ambushed by another tribe, attack was often the only appropriate response. But in other circumstances—a cold, stormy night for example, or perhaps a situation in which the woods were overrun with enemies unaware of your hiding place—a sort of biological shutdown was the appropriate behavior. Primitive man often had to cope with cold. His body's response was to constrict peripheral blood vessels and capillaries to conserve heat. His basal metabolism slowed down and his body went into a quasi-somnolent state. In these kinds of circumstances our great-great ancestor sort of hibernated. This was a stress response, just as adaptive to survival as dashing away from danger or bashing an attacker's head in with a club. Withdrawal was the behavior appropriate to surviving a stormy night. Indeed, after his amazing run from the Blackfoot Indians, John Colter had to survive that night hidden in a driftwood pile, naked, with bone-chilling water gurgling by just inches below him. Hidden in a log pile, with enemies all around, reduced breathing, minimal heartbeat, inactivity, and just enough heat production to keep from dying of hypothermia was the best course for ancient ancestor and for John Colter.

To be sure, a withdrawal response to either a saber-tooth

tiger or an attacking Neanderthal would have proven disastrous one million years ago, just as running about naked in freezing weather would have been lethal. Thus we evolved, with a mix of psychological and physiological stress reactions designed to help us survive different kinds of threats.

Unfortunately we've only been "modern men" for a few brief years in contrast to our species' tenure on this globe, and we've been industrialized, cultured, and "civilized" men for but a flyspeck in time compared to our natural history.

John Colter's stress responses were appropriate to escaping Indians, yet a similar chain of responses when meeting with the vice-president in charge of finance is not in your best interest. There you are, in your business suit, necktie, polished shoes . . . with a pounding pulse, shortness of breath, increased blood pressure, and muscles twitching and itching for accelerated physical activity. For all that, you are expected to appear rational, calm, in charge of yourself.

"I believe I can explain this, Mr. Blackfoot. You see we've been anticipating a jump in costs during the year ahead, so we wanted to prepare this year . . ."

In our primitive past, fight and flight reactions were fundamental to survival:

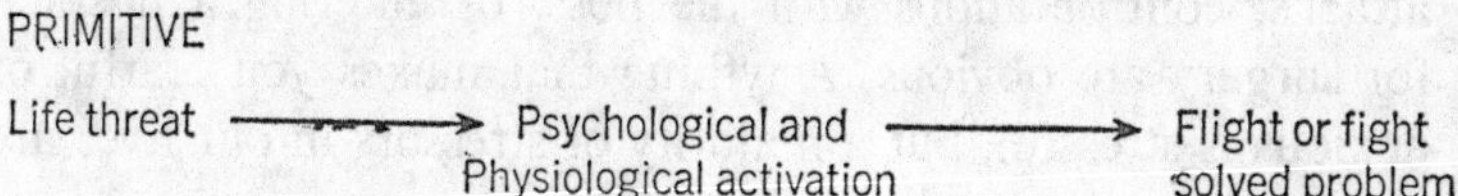

Human though it is, fight and flight response is not the best behavior in old Blackfoot's office:

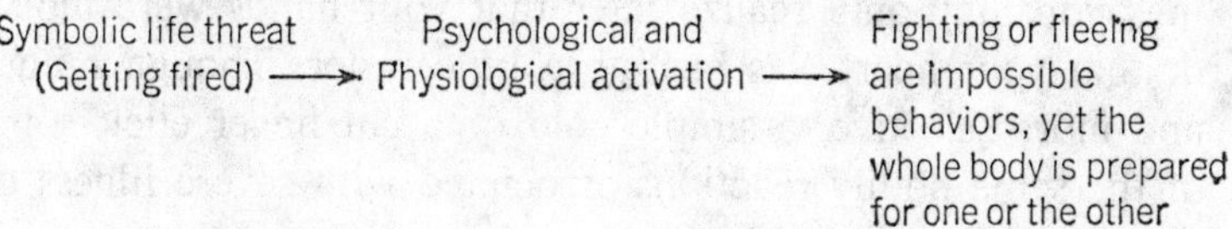

"You are on thin ice," says Blackfoot. "I want a turnabout in the next fiscal quarter, or I'm going to have some heads. And another thing. Stop that damn fidgeting. I can't stand people who twitch and fidget."

The worst part is that Blackfoot may not actually say all this; he may only be thinking it. Or only you may be thinking it!

Alas, withdrawal in contemporary society can be even more disastrous than fidgeting.

"Damn it," says Blackfoot, "say something. How can we solve this problem if you keep staring out that window? Are you having some kind of nervous breakdown?"

Perhaps you are.

Ten thousand years ago, in a hollow log, withdrawal could have saved your life. Today, in Blackfoot's office, withdrawal just lost you your job:

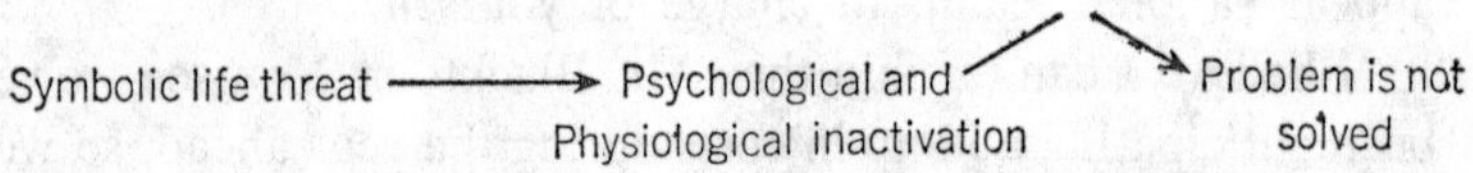

The insidious aspect of stressors is that they are not always so obvious as the dogs Dr. Cannon introduced to his experimental cats. Certainly such stress-producing events as physical attacks, confrontations with the boss, or entering a hospital for surgery are obvious. Anything that makes you fearful or anxious is stressful, but a majority of stressors in our lives are more subtle.

Driving an automobile can be terribly stressful, as can college tests, monotonous work, a mild rebuff, or waiting in line. These kinds of stressors may trigger such relatively low-profile physical reactions they go almost unnoticed. In business dealings you may only realize later that your hands were moist, or that your heart was beating a little faster. Though milder and more selective, a simple cold or a cut finger elicit some of the same bodily reactions associated with severe illness or massive tissue damage.

Among Hans Selye's profound contributions to understanding stress was the discovery that the body's stress reactions can exhaust themselves if overworked. For instance, bacterial infection causes the body to manufacture additional white blood cells, which in turn destroy invading bacteria. Over time, however, the defense mechanism can become exhausted if the invading bacteria persist. Then the patient succumbs to his illness.

John Colter could not have run forever. Historical accounts of his astonishing feat suggest he was at the threshold of physical collapse. Another few hundred yards of running would likely have seen the end of his effective stress responses. He then would have fallen exhausted.

Poor Colter. After surviving his ordeal with the Blackfoot Indians in 1809, and another skirmish or two with them that same year, he fled the mountains in early spring of 1810, announcing, upon his leave-taking: "If God will only forgive me this time and let me off I will leave this Godforsaken country day after tomorrow . . . and be damned if I ever come into it again."

Colter had come from frontier Virginia, originally. He joined Lewis and Clark in 1803 when twenty-eight years old. On that grand trip of discovery in '04–5 he proved himself among the ablest, bravest, and brightest of the expeditionaries. Later he was to be the first white man to see the wonders of the Yellowstone country, and indeed he was the first mountain man to have laid eyes on countless valleys, ridge tops, forests, and icy streams. He accomplished enough to earn lasting distinction as a geographical explorer, yet by the end of his life he was counted among the heroic liars of his era. Only years later were his "tall tales" substantiated, virtually all of them.

John left the mountains for St. Louis in 1810, arriving that May. He bought a small farm on the banks of the Missouri, found himself a bride, and within two years was dead of infectious illness.

Life is a wearing-down process. An arrow can hurry the job along. So can freezing rains, a rock slide, an angry grizzly bear. But what finally overtook John Colter was stress—stress that was not so readily apparent.

CHAPTER 3

THE MIND-BODY NONSENSE

Our medical traditions divide diseases into two camps. The terms "mental," "emotional," "functional," and "psychogenic" are used to describe one division of illnesses. The words "organic," "physical," and "somatogenic" are used to describe the other. This time-honored tradition of separating mental and physical health may be the single greatest deterrent to quality health care in our culture.

DAY-TO-DAY PUZZLES

A typical newspaper report describes a medical research project announced by one of the Midwest's prestigious medical schools. CATCHING SOMEONE'S COLD ISN'T SO EASY states the front-page headline.[1] The short article reports a research project in which husbands or wives were experimentally infected with a cold virus, one of some 150 known viruses that produce common cold symptoms. Then the infected subjects' spouses were observed.

[1] San Francisco *Chronicle,* February 3, 1976. The study was formally reported in the Journal of Infectious Diseases, January 1976.

The couples were together an average of some 122 hours during the experiment, more than 17 hours a day. The results came as a "surprise" to the researchers. Only 38 per cent of the infected cold sufferers transmitted their colds to a husband or wife. The research project's group leader was startled. Said he, "It is difficult to understand why cold viruses are not more easily transmitted from person to person considering the fact that it takes only about one virus particle deliberately put into the nasal passages to produce an experimental infection."

According to the paper, the study has encouraging implications. "If the virus is not easily transmitted from one person to another, it might be possible to find relatively simple ways of making the transmission even more difficult." Perhaps some mechanical or antiseptic device to break the chain of transmission? The newspaper article concludes "that the study results did confirm (the researcher's) impression that the person-to-person spread of virus is unpredictable and difficult to detect even though respiratory virus infections are widespread in the whole community."

In this interview our researcher tells us that a single virus can initiate cold symptoms, and yet in a world (let alone in an experiment) in which cold viruses are swarming, it's hard to catch a cold. Despite the paradox raised by his own experiment, the researcher tenaciously clings to a direct cause-and-effect explanation for colds. One virus, one cold.

Representing another side of the problem, a recent editorial comment in *Time* magazine by a medical professor at Yale urged that we should remember the disease *anorexia nervosa* might be caused by "organic" problems, since only then could anorexia patients and their families avoid the "shame" and "guilt" of having a disease of psychiatric origin.[2]

[2] The "starvation disease" or "Twiggy syndrome," a rare disorder in which one becomes obsessed with losing weight. The result is abnormal weight loss and malnutrition. Sometimes patients simply stop eating. The professor's letter was written in response to an article about a seventeen-year-old girl who was five feet five inches tall and whose weight had dropped to seventy pounds.

Christ, for one, made no such distinction between organic and psychic diseases. In his view all illness was the result of sin. Likewise, in Jewish tradition all illness was regarded as sinful, a certain sign of bad blood or bad parents. The ancient Greeks believed any illness was a sign of weakness. Our society tends to modify these views. We only punish those labeled with a psychiatric illness. Any of us branded as having a mental illness may find it difficult to land a job. Once employed, managements are reluctant to promote or advance someone with a history of psychiatric disease. Neighbors and friends shy away from a psychiatric patient, even years after the illness is cured. Remember McGovern's first running mate in the presidential election of 1972? Senator Thomas Eagleton dropped out of the race after it was *disclosed* he had been treated for *mental illness!* A graduate of Harvard Law School, Tom Eagleton was elected attorney general of Missouri at the age of thirty-one. He was governor of Missouri four years later. His subsequent record as a United States senator was honorable, yet in mid-career he was not allowed to run for the office of vice president because, quoting a 1972 newspaper headline, TOP DEMOS THINK EAGLETON HAMPERS BEAT-NIXON DRIVE BECAUSE OF PREVIOUSLY UNDISCLOSED PSYCHIATRIC TREATMENT.[3]

In contrast, no similar penalties or haunting doubts exist for other illnesses, a broken leg for example. Time off from work is generously granted without stigma. Friends and neighbors organize the next party at the patient's house so "poor old Fred" won't have to walk a block. Fred's fractured leg is viewed by all as an unavoidable accident. (He fell from a cherry tree he was pruning.) Fred's bum leg is curable, proper, even sort of amusing. Just look at all the autographs and limericks written on Fred's plaster cast.

[3] Fortunately for Tom Eagleton and the country, Missouri's voters display better sense than some "top Demos." Senator Eagleton continues to serve, with distinction, in Washington, D.C. It's ironic that Senator Eagleton's treatment was for the same psychiatric disease that Abraham Lincoln almost certainly suffered from according to historians—manic depressive illness.

Fred is forty-six, a hard-working stockbroker, father of three children who are variously off to colleges, marriages, and careers. This is not Fred's first broken bone.

Fred's doctor first saw him thirty-two years ago when Fred was just fourteen. He had skittered around a corner too quickly on his bicycle, lost control, and spilled. The resulting broken forearm brought Fred in for an X ray and cast.

A year or two later Fred's collar bone was fractured in a bruising sandlot football game with some older, bigger boys.

By the time he was in college Fred was an excellent skier, without mishap until he took a jump off an advanced ski-jump hill against the sound advice of his companions. The resulting knee, back, and hip injuries put Fred in the hospital for the next two months; in assorted casts and orthopedic braces for the following year. For all that, he was lucky. When he hit those tree tops at the side of the jump hill, his friends were certain he'd been killed.

Good luck, of sorts, rode with Fred. In his senior year of college he rolled his car over a bridge abutment, and everyone agreed it was a miracle he escaped with only three cracked ribs.

Upon graduation, Fred joined the staff of a brokerage firm and did very well during the post-Korean War stock market heyday. In 1956 he married, bought a house in the suburbs, and soon was a father. Two months after his first daughter was born, Fred fractured several knuckles and fingers on both hands, a freak accident. As he explained it to his doctor, while repairing a spring-suspended, overhead garage door, one of the springs broke, pinning his hands beneath the heavy falling door. It was a miserable few weeks, but Fred's orthopedic surgeon repaired the hands.

Just about everyone who visits Hawaii is tempted to ride a surf board, and in 1963 when Fred and his wife vacationed on Oahu, Fred took surfing lessons until he was quite competent. The old skiing co-ordination seemed to come right back. Several days after his lessons, in a modest surf off Sunset Beach,

Fred *wiped out*. In surfing parlance that means falling off your board dramatically. In Fred's wipeout, the surf board, with a ton or so of water behind it, slapped him across the lower face . . . . fracturing his jaw, smashing his nose, and dislodging a half-dozen teeth.

Passing quickly over Fred's elbow fracture in 1965 (while attempting a victory leap over a tennis net), his ruptured disc in 1967 (precipitated by his singlehandedly moving a refrigerator), and the wrist he cracked in 1971 (when an automobile jack malfunctioned), medical records show that Fred had seven other orthopedic hand and foot injuries between 1965 and 1975. All of these injuries were diagnosed and treated as specific and acute problems.

Yes, Fred's doctor knows he has an unusual case of accident-proneness on his hands. He even suspects that the recurring hand and feet injuries might be the result of Fred's habit of venting anger and frustration by pounding his hands and feet against trees, garage doors, automobiles, and walls. Still, the attending doctor only treats Fred's acute problems. To suggest that Fred might have a chronic illness, let alone a "mental" illness would perhaps be bad taste. And imagine what Fred's business associates might think!

LINGUISTIC PARALLELISM

Essayist Annie Dillard recalls her childhood belief that all foreign languages were codes for English. Not until her first day in French class did she realize, with dismay, that she would have to learn speech all over again, one word at a time. In myriad ways, the medical community views illness with equivalent naïveté, a kind of pre-French class innocence.

Consider an ulcer patient. The clinical psychiatrist recognizes a psychiatric cause for the disease and pursues a course of therapy designed to change the patient's attitudes and behaviors that are encouraging an excess flow of stomach acids. The internist recognizes a malfunction in the digestive system and prescribes modifications in diet. The surgeon recognizes an organic disorder and considers removing the ulcer by knife. All three physicians appreciate the methodologies of their colleagues, but basically they consider the other procedures to be ancillary, mere adjuncts to their own procedures.

Barbara B. Brown points to a paradox between what she calls feeling man and laboratory man. Psychologists and physiologists take experimental knowledge into research laboratories and dissect it down into bits of chemistry, physics, or animal instinct. Thus has laboratory man pursued what makes the heart function mechanically for 1,800 years; yet when he, the scientist, discovers some new information about the heart's physical action, he fails to notice that his own heart is racing with the excitement of his own mind's discovery. Dr. Brown observes that we feel and experience body changes with every mind activity, yet "formal knowledge neither admits of nor recognizes virtually any connection between mind and body not explainable by old Newtonian cause and effect laws of physics."

To an observer from an advanced world, says Dr. Brown, "seeing through us and around us with all-knowing vision," our scientific community might appear to be suffering from hysterical blindness, a refusal to see how we might rise above "the security of the empirical womb we believe we live in."

No scientist has done a better job of analyzing this medical and scientific paradox than David T. Graham who describes what he calls *linguistic parallelism* in health, disease, and the mind-body problem. We've evolved two separate medical vocabularies he points out. Actually, says Dr. Graham, few physicians disagree with the idea that the mind and body influence each other. Still, such endorsements are mostly glib; seldom are they incorporated into medical practice, medical writing, or medical thinking. Why does this dualistic view persist? Because it *does* represent reality. There is a duality of "psychic" and "physical," however the duality is not of the events observed, but of the language used to describe them. Dr. Graham provides an illustration. Consider these two statements:

"John Smith was frightened when he saw the cat."

"When light rays from the cat reached John Smith's retina, various biochemical processes were set up that resulted in the passage of impulses over the optic nerve to the occipital cortex, with activation of sympathetic hypothalmic nuclei, and increased activity in sympathetic nerves to the heart, leading to tachycardia."[4]

These represent two ways to describe the same event, just as "mind" and "body" are two ways of labeling the same thing.

Fred's doctor might readily admit to a psychiatric basis for Fred's accident-proneness. But what does he do about it? By employing the vocabulary of orthopedics, he never even raises the question.

Doctors seldom treat the "whole man," despite the comfortable old adage to do so. Few physicians have the time or energy to consider what the whole man might be. In many ways, the current fashion for doctors to "specialize" has brought the average practitioner further away from the whole man than ever. Even our health organizations have become specialized. We support, for example, a National Institute of Mental Health. Medical literature repeatedly contains references to "sound minds" and "sound bodies." In both the popular and medical press the phrase "psychiatrists and physicians" is familiar.

So ingrained is the mind-body myth into our thinking we totally embrace fatuous beliefs. For example, we commonly accept the idea that alcohol and heroin are "addictive," hence when "physical withdrawal" is accomplished the patient is cured. In contrast, we all accept the idea that tobacco is "only habituating," since "psychic not physical dependence" is developed. These are cherished notions, upheld by no less than the World Health Organization. Some drugs capture our minds

[4] In this example the lexicon of psychology is more convenient than that of physiology, but that is by no means always the case.

and some our bodies. Habituation versus addiction. Linguistic parallelism.[5]

In another newspaper item, an Associated Press release on Gerald Ford's physical condition, the President's physician stated that Ford faced six problems in 1975 that might have affected his health, but he surmounted all of them. (For example, two assassination attempts.)

In a written report, the President's doctor said, "The President suffered no ill effects either physically or emotionally." More linguistic parallelism.

Perhaps the best evidence of how inexorably your mind and body are linked, in fact, is your own insight based on everyday experience. For instance, consider your answers to these easy questions:

Do you notice any "physical" reactions when someone sneaks up behind you and shouts, "Boo?"

What normally stirs you sexually?

Why are you not sexually aroused all the time?

Do you experience "physical changes" when you are angry, sad, happy, or frightened?

Does your "mood" change when you are exhausted, cold, or in pain?

Answers to such questions easily demonstrate how the mind triggers all manner of bodily changes and how bodily changes can influence the mind. Yet culturally we find it terribly difficult to alter our language, thinking, or judgments about the mind-body. We still take our "emotional" problems to "psychiatrists" and our "physical" complaints to "physicians." The medical community continues to divide itself into meth-

[5] *Addiction* is customarily held to be a physiological dependence on some agent with a tendency to increase its use. *Habituation* is customarily held to be psychological dependence on the use of some agent with little or no tendency to increase its use. In reality these definitions do not hold up. For instance, some medical experts recognize both "psychological addiction" and "physiological addiction" to alcohol. As any cigarette smoker who has stopped can testify, the physical discomfort upon quitting is severe, even painful. And, in fact, "addicts" frequently do not increase their dose of a dependency agent while "habituates" frequently do.

odological camps. True, such separation may be of no great lasting consequence in dealing with colds and cut fingers. But what of serious illness? How about a patient with severe heart disease or serious schizophrenia?

Let's look at the psychopathology of a patient with chronic obstructive lung disease, an emphysema victim. Here the mind-body problem can be deadly and cruel.

THE WHOLE PATIENT

The usual psychopathology of emphysema follows two courses, both of them maladaptive. At first the patient is depressed, angry and/or frightened about his condition. The anger and fright make him breathe faster, but because his lungs are deteriorated they cannot accommodate the speeded-up breathing and he starts gasping for breath. This only increases the patient's fright, which in turn increases his breathing, which aggravates the gasping . . . a grim, escalating cycle which may lead to complete respiratory collapse.

Most emphysema patients, sooner or later, begin to realize the relationship between emotions and gasping attacks. They then begin to fear *any* kind of emotion. Our patient adopts defense mechanisms to protect himself against all feelings of joy, excitement, sadness, or fear. The result is isolation, denial, and repression. "Good Lord," people say. "First it was lung problems and now he's mentally ill."

To treat emphysema, or any other severe chronic illness, without total regard for the patient ("take these every day and come back in six weeks") is, at best, a half-baked response to the disease. At worst, it leads to miserable or prematurely dead patients.

Ideally, our emphysema patient's physician would use some scientific instrument like the life change scale (presented in Chapter 5) to help the patient recognize and quantify events and experiences in his life that are stressful. Thus informed, the patient could knowledgeably and consciously adjust his behavior to reduce breathing attacks. In helping the patient understand what factors precipitate attacks, as well as advice on how to cope with working adjustments, sexual adjustments, and family adjustments, his responses to all forms of treatment will be more effective. To control or improve the emphysema patient's condition, the whole patient must be treated.

Mending Fred's broken bones and sending him home is not treating the whole patient. Nor is it "curing" Fred.

Just as shortsighted is a purely psychiatric view which too often forgets that the "physical" problems–broken bones, an eroded stomach, shortness of breath, pounding heart–are painful, serious, and real. For that matter, even "psychiatric" problems are sometimes treated in a cavalier fashion by "mind doctors." The following dialogue is amusing at first reading:

PATIENT: I feel depressed.

DOCTOR: Tell me more about such feelings.

PATIENT: I don't know why I feel depressed.

DOCTOR: Why don't you know why you feel depressed?

PATIENT: I just don't know why.

DOCTOR: Please go on.

PATIENT: Can you give me a hint?

DOCTOR: You believe I can give you a hint, don't you?

PATIENT: Yes I do.

DOCTOR: Can you be more informative?

PATIENT: Are you a doctor?

DOCTOR: Why are you interested in whether I am a doctor or not?

PATIENT: I need help.

DOCTOR: What would it mean to you if you got help?

PATIENT: I would feel better.

DOCTOR: What does that suggest to you?

PATIENT: If you are a doctor then you should be able to help me.

DOCTOR: Do you think it's likely that if I am a doctor then I should be able to help me?

PATIENT: I am still depressed.

DOCTOR: Is it because you are still depressed that you came to me?

PATIENT: What can you do about it?

DOCTOR: What do you think?

PATIENT: Help.

DOCTOR: Earlier you said you were still depressed.

PATIENT: I am still depressed.

DOCTOR: I am sorry to hear you are depressed.

PATIENT: Can you help me get out of this depressed state?

DOCTOR: When have you asked such questions before?

PATIENT: Yesterday.

DOCTOR: What else would you like to discuss?

To be sure, no trained psychiatrist would treat a patient this way, but a computer programmed to play psychiatrist did.[6] Unfortunately some physicians are similarly programmed to look at patients and diseases in only one way.

WHO RECOVERS FROM SURGERY?

Few medical procedures appear more pragmatic than open-heart surgery. Here life and death seem to balance solely on the surgeon's skill. But it isn't so.

A study conducted by Dr. Chase Kimball in 1968, at the University of Rochester Medical School, assigned open-heart surgery patients to one of four categories, depending on the patients' attitudes and characteristics. These were determined by interviewing the patients before their operations. Fifty-four patients were thus interviewed consecutively as they entered the hospital for surgery.

Group I were described as "adjusted." They were reality-oriented and purposeful, they coped well with stressors, in-

[6] This particular computer game is called "Doctor." It was programmed for academic exercise and amusement, by Joseph Weisenbaum at MIT. Dr. Weisenbaum is bemused when others take it seriously. Incredibly, some scientists have seriously attempted to write programs to "psychoanalyze," which again points to how psychiatric sciences are viewed in our society. It's unlikely these same programmers would have a computer perform brain surgery.

cluding their diseases. Even though ill, they had continued to successfully conduct business and domestic affairs. They viewed the impending surgery as desirable and necessary. They could express uneasiness, fear, and anxiety about the surgery, but they were in control and insightful. They acknowledged that death was a possibility, but they were basically optimistic that the operation would be a success.

Group II were described as "symbiotic." This group had adapted well to their illnesses, to the point where they were achieving gains being sick. They had considerable dependence on a parent or spouse. Their cardiac symptoms were often precipitated by feelings of being threatened. This group approached surgery with a view of maintaining the status quo. They didn't really want to improve, nor did they want to get worse. They didn't wish the future to hold anything different than the best of the past.

Group III were described as "denying anxiety." Symptoms and signs of their illnesses were denied or minimized. They did manifest uneasiness about the surgery, but they couldn't verbalize it. Instead, they appeared rigid, hyperalert, suspicious, and hyperactive. Many were sleepless and had no appetite. Their relationship with the hospital staff was stilted, and they were unable to talk about death.

Group IV were described as "depressed." They gave varying pictures of previously coping with stressful events. Some had suffered lifelong sagas of disappointments and hardships. Over a prolonged period they had first "given in" and then finally "given up" in their efforts to live with their diseases. Others had successful lives, but experienced a deterioration of psychological adjustment at the onset or exacerbation of their cardiac symptoms. At the time of surgery all of these patients were clinically depressed. They denied anxiety about the operation. They didn't care what happened. Their motivation for surgery was characteristically verbalized as "the doctors thought I should have it." Most of the patients felt hopeless, saying such things as, "It's no use; nothing they can do will help."

Among all four groups of patients, comparisons of age, length or severity of illness, and duration of the operation were not significant.

Among thirteen patients in Group I, one died because of a mechanical mishap. Nine improved in health. Three remained more or less unchanged.

Among fifteen patients in Group II, one died and one improved. The rest remained unchanged or got worse.

Among twelve patients in Group III, four died, three of them during surgery. Three improved, three remained unchanged, and two became worse.

Among fifteen patients in Group IV, eleven died. Eleven of the fifteen! Almost 80 per cent of the depressed patients didn't survive.

RESULTS OF OPEN-HEART SURGERY FOR 54 PATIENTS MEASURED 3 TO 15 MONTHS AFTER SURGERY*

	Group I (Adjusted)	Group II (Symbiotic)	Group III (Anxious)	Group IV (Depressed)
Number of Patients	13	15	12	15
Unchanged	3	8	3	2
Improved	9	1	3	1
Worse	0	5	2	1
Dead	1	1	4	11

* Adapted from "A predictive study of adjustment to cardiac surgery," by Chase Patterson Kimball, M.D., *Journal of Thoracic and Cardiovascular Surgery,* December 1969.

These groups were identified before surgery, and the major differences between them were their attitudes. Here then is evidence that the common cold, broken bones, and response to open-heart surgery have a common bond, that is, a relationship to some complex interplay between the individual and the environment. To understand this relationship it is first necessary to abandon the mind-body myth and think of yourself as a wholly integrated psychobiologic system.

Catching the common cold may not be easy, but dying during heart surgery appears to be an odds-on probability if you go into surgery *not caring about the outcome.*

pings included thirty-two reports of people who dropped dead in the face of danger. Some of these represented direct and urgent threats, such as personal assaults, shipwrecks, and earthquakes; others resulted from indirect (but no less urgent) traumas. For example, a hold-up suspect who died in court while describing how "scared" he was performing the hold-up, or a woman who died while phoning the police to report a beating and robbery under way in front of her house.

As Dr. Engel points out, dying of a "broken heart" or "being scared to death" are points of view laymen have long accepted more readily than doctors. Poets and playwrights have discerned such realities in the pattern of human drama for centuries.

But what of joy?

Perhaps Dr. Engel's most surprising news items reported people who died on happy occasions. Three died during reunions after long separations. One tragic report described a fifty-five-year-old man reunited with his eighty-eight-year-old father after a separation of more than twenty years. Both collapsed and died at the moment of their meeting! Another report described a man who won over sixteen hundred dollars on a two-dollar race-track bet. He died while collecting his payoff.

From interviews with thousands of patients, Dr. Engel identified five characteristics that typify the *Giving-Up Given-Up Complex* and its role in preceding illness: 1) feelings of helplessness or hopelessness that lead to an attitude of giving up; 2) feelings of reduced self-worth, a depreciated self-image; 3) a loss of gratification from life's relationships and roles, a result of either real or imagined failures, rebuffs, loss of standing, decline of ability or strength, a thwarting of life's goals; 4) a disruption in a sense of time continuity, a feeling that one's past, present, and future is in danger of interruption, that devices used in the past will no longer work in the future, which holds little or no promise; 5) a reminder of times past when feelings of helplessness and hopelessness prevailed, virtually a reliving of grim times simply by thinking back, even though they are in the past and no longer relevant to day-to-day living.[1]

"In essence," says Dr. Engel, ". . . during such a state the total biologic economy of the organism is altered, at times in such a way that its capability to deal with certain potentially pathogenic processes is reduced, permitting disease to develop." Your emotions, in other words, can reduce your normal ability to avoid illness.

Continuing, Dr. Engel writes:

> Finally, to call attention to the biological side of this psychobiological reaction, let me point out that there is ample evidence in modern neurophysiology and neuroendocrinology to show that it is precisely when the central nervous system is failing in its task of processing input that emergency biologic defense systems are invoked. Such failure results when an input relevant to the organism's adjustment is too great (overload) or when no program or response to the input is available (incongruence); or, in psychological terms, when information cannot be handled promptly and effectively by mental mechanisms alone. Under such circumstances the organism has available no relevant behavior.

Dr. Engel is describing what might be called biological and psychological short circuits. In the attic of your house or walls of your apartment, an electrical short circuit may cause a fire or explosion. In the infinitely more complex system of your body, imagine what short circuits or overloads produce among millions of cells, hundreds of thousands of biochemical reactions, and near-limitless numbers of neural and chemical feed-

[1] Such an important point! Even when your present situation is relaxed, pleasant, and healthy, you can still misdirect those fathomless instruments—your imagination and memory—to make yourself sick. It's so easy to foul a good day by conjuring from memory the past's bad days. Or to sandbag a personal relationship by comparing it with past relationships.

back systems—a "circuitry" that makes the most complex computer system toylike by comparison.

HELPLESSNESS

Hardly anyone argues with the idea that stressful circumstances over time are injurious to your health, but Dr. Engel's observations illuminate a chilling fact: even one stressful event, if of sufficient impact, can be devastating. When emotional trauma is so overwhelming as to create a feeling of absolute despair, it may totally defeat your normal coping mechanisms. In a dramatic, experimental demonstration of this, a psychologist at Johns Hopkins, Dr. Curt Richter, in the mid-1950s demonstrated the effects of "giving up," using wild rats.

Wild rats are normally excellent swimmers. Dr. Richter tossed one into a tank of water where it thrashed for sixty hours before finally succumbing to exhaustion. Then, Richter held a second rat in his hand for several minutes until it stopped struggling to escape. When tossed into water, the second rat sank to the bottom and drowned within minutes. The rat's will to survive short-circuited before it hit the water. The rat gave up in Richter's hand.

What do rats have to do with us?

Dr. Richter was demonstrating why voodoo spells sometimes work. When the person upon whom a voodoo spell is cast believes in a voodoo death, the belief alone can be lethal. Like the second rat, the voodoo victim gives up and dies.

Martin Seligman, associate professor of psychology at the University of Pennsylvania, labels such incidents "psychogenic, sudden, and mysterious death." He relates an example told to him by Major F. Harold Kushner, an army medical officer who was held by the Vietcong for almost six years. In Kushner's POW camp there was a tough twenty-four-year-old Marine, who had survived two years of imprisonment in good health, largely, it seemed to Kushner, because the camp's commander had promised the Marine release if he co-operated.

The Marine was a model prisoner, but as time went by he began to understand that the commander had lied to him. As the realization sank in, his behavior changed. He suddenly refused to work and rejected all offers of food or encouragement. He just lay on his cot. Within weeks he was dead. A strictly medical explanation of the Marine's death isn't adequate, says Seligman. The psychological shock of realizing his actions were wasted and futile destroyed his motivation to remain alive.

Consider old age. Dr. Seligman points to a study in which a researcher interviewed women, average age eighty-two, who were about to enter a nursing home. Asked how much freedom of choice they felt they had, thirty-eight of the group said they had some while seventeen said they had no choice. At the end of just ten weeks after entering the home, only one of the thirty-eight who felt they had options had died; however, sixteen of the choiceless group were dead.

The elderly are subjected to more helplessness and hopelessness than just about any other segment of our society. Often forced to retire at sixty-five, ignored by their children, taxed out of their houses, packed off to nursing homes, the elderly frequently have very little choice in their destinies. "We are a nation that deprives old persons of control over their lives," writes Seligman in his book *Helplessness*. "We kill them."

Recall the poignant lines from Paul Simon's song "Old Friends":

Can you imagine us
Years from today,
Sharing a park bench quietly?
How terribly strange
To be seventy.

Old friends,
Memory brushes the same years.
Silently sharing the same fear . . .

A statistician with the Wessex Regional Health Authority in Hampshire, England, has found a modest but consistent relationship between death and birthdays for people seventy-five and older. Michael Alderson obtained statistics on all of the people who died in England and Wales during 1972 and tabulated their birth and death dates. He found that elderly people were less likely to die in the months just before their birthdays and more likely to die in the months afterward. In exploring possible causes for this, the *British Medical Journal* speculated that "In old age, each birthday is an achievement, a source of esteem, evidence that the old man or woman has cheated death for another year." Pointing to our role in *deciding* when we die, the *British Medical Journal* reported an old woman in Wales who was told she would die before Christmas. She wagered her minister that she could prove her doctor wrong. And she did. On Christmas Day she demanded her payoff. Then she died. If old people are able to stay alive for the sake of something so trivial as a wager or birthday, "then it should not be too difficult to help them find other reasons," states the journal.

This is a crucial issue for the elderly, one exemplified by a famous British study entitled *Broken Heart,* in which the death rates for 4,500 widowers were followed for nine years after the deaths of their wives. Two hundred of these men died within six months of their wives' deaths, a mortality rate 40 per cent higher than for married men of the same ages. More startling yet was the fact that one fourth of these men died of the same diseases that killed their wives.

Perhaps, suggests the *British Medical Journal,* such death rates would be reduced if we could offer help to men and women under severe stress. If people themselves play a role in deciding when they are going to die, couldn't we help them decide in favor of life?

Lines from another song, "Hello in There," by John Prine, seem to punctuate the plight of the elderly:

You know old trees just grow stronger
Old rivers grow wider every day
But old people they just grow lonesome
Waitin' for someone to say
Hello in there
Hello

AT LAST AN EXPLANATION FOR THE COMMON COLD?

From earliest childhood we learn that germs lurk everywhere, pernicious, deadly, ready to destroy us the moment we let up our guard. Certainly pasteurization, plumbing, contemporary hygiene, and vaccinations, have reduced our exposure to infectious bacteria and viruses but have by no means banished them from the scene. Germs, despite precautions, are still found everywhere. Even today, approximately 1 per cent of surgical patients acquire postoperative infection. Somehow the enemy slips through a Maginot line of detergents, soaps, steaming devices, antiseptics, microspore-filtering air systems, and exhaust pumps employed by modern hospitals to banish infectious agents from operating rooms. If such potent precautions occasionally fail there, imagine what we all are exposed to daily. Consider the bacteria exchanged during a handshake or a kiss! Why aren't we falling like flies?

One reason is that very few bacteria among the world's gargantuan population of them are actually harmful to us. What's more, among those that give us trouble, in a majority of instances, *it is our reactions to the bacteria that make us sick, not the bacteria themselves.*

In his inspired and thoughtful book *Lives of a Cell,* Lewis Thomas shares this insight with us:

"Our arsenals for fighting off bacteria are so powerful, and involve so many different defense mechanisms, that we are in more danger from them than from the invaders."

By way of one example, Dr. Thomas points to staphylococci, a bacteria that has adapted to conditions on our skin, an environment that most other bacteria find intolerable. Staphylococci dwell all over us, yet we have remarkably little difficulty with them. Only a few of us are vexed by boils, the result of our own leukocytes trying to destroy the staphylococci. Most of the resulting tissue damage is accomplished by the leukocytes. In their assault on the staphylococci they get out of control. They short-circuit. Such defense mechanisms are reacting to primitive memory, says Dr. Thomas, something evolved millions of years ago. "We live in the midst of explosive devices; we are mined."

Why do such primitive mine fields go off sometimes and not other times; why do some of us suffer from boils while others do not?

A study was conducted in 1950 of illness among a division of telephone operators in New York City, two thousand women in all. Approximately 25 per cent of these women contributed to 75 per cent of the division's sickness for the year. When examined, medical records showed that roughly the same 25 per cent had accounted for most of the sick leave in preceding years. As it turned out, these patterns of illness were uniform for periods of up to twenty years. Why did germs, among other woes, pick mainly on just 25 per cent of these women?[2] In hopes of finding a clue, the researchers looked for differences in the personal lives between the two groups of workers.

The high-illness group was made up of women "who could not satisfy what they considered to be their needs in the situation in which they found themselves." Most were not satisfied with their educational backgrounds. Many had been pressed into their present job because of financial realities. All had been thwarted in the attempt to seek advancement in one form or another. Most had strong sexual drives, but for a wide

[2] The high-illness group experienced more of all types of illness, including surgical operations and injuries. As a group they were especially subject to chronic and recurring headaches, respiratory infections, intestinal problems, menstrual pain, high blood pressure, and obesity.

range of reasons—widowhood, divorce, strict religious beliefs—they found themselves in sexually unrewarding circumstances with no obvious means of escape. Collectively, the high-illness group were known by their fellow workers as people who were ambitious, hard to get along with, complaining. Their behaviors, attitudes, and bodily reactions were "modified by their attempts to adapt to these situations and to satisfy their frustrated needs."

In contrast, the low-illness group were essentially satisfied with their positions in life. They enjoyed their associations with fellow workers, had modest sex drives, and not much interest in assuming more responsibility. They exhibited little conflict over personal or social problems. As a group, they also seemed to be able to make themselves comfortable in most situations.

Dull? Perhaps, but healthier than the women with similar lives who felt frustrated, thwarted, and unhappy with their circumstances.

In your school, office, factory, professional group, club associations, or circle of friends, look at those among you who normally enjoy good health. Compare them to those among you who seem to suffer a range of health problems. Who catch colds? Virtually all of us are exposed to the circumstances that initiate cold symptoms. The "cold" we normally describe—runny nose, cough, swollen lymph glands, sneezing, fever—is actually the body's overreaction, in most cases, to a bacterial or viral threat. The common cold may be, more than anything else, a biological short circuit.

"Sometimes," writes Dr. Thomas, "the mechanisms used for overkill are immunologic, but often . . . they are more primitive kinds of memory. We tear ourselves to pieces because of symbols, and we are more vulnerable to this than a host of predators."

As far back as 1948, studies by Harold G. Wolff and his colleagues at Cornell showed that many of the symptoms associated with colds and other respiratory ailments could be triggered in experimental situations by exposing test subjects to emotional stressors.

Ammonia fumes or pollen normally precipitate a pattern of swelling and secretion by nasal tissues, along with tears, coughing, and sneezing. In repeated studies, similar reactions were elicited in subjects merely by the suggestion of circumstances or events; being reminded of an unhappy marriage, for instance, or reminded of personal situations which made the subjects feel angry, fearful, bitter, or helpless. Since Wolff's original studies, it has been demonstrated repeatedly that changes in nasal functions associated with emotional conflict often produce tears, runny noses, and even pathological tissue changes. In a person whose emotional conflict is unresolved, the nasal symptoms frequently become recurring and chronic. Monday morning's sinuses. The nervous sniffle.

Among the day-to-day problems, triumphs, and events we all experience, there is an infinite range of stressors. From bitter coffee at dawn to unresolved problems at dusk, from great personal achievements to life's tragedies, all of us must cope with a constant mix of stressful events, minor and major. Some are joyful and many are not.

Trapped in jobs we want to escape, or locked into contracts that seem to bind, or graced by life patterns that breed euphoria, too many of us subsequently overreact, underreact, or react inappropriately, thus providing the stage setting in which illness occurs. In this context, Christmas can initiate your common cold. The death of a President may kill you. Short circuits in either case.

Enough morbid anecdotes and statistics. Let's move on to what all this can mean to your health.

CHAPTER 5

THE IMPACT OF LIFE CHANGE

Preventive medicine is like the weather Charles Dudley Warner described—everybody talks about it, but nobody does anything about it. The apparent reason is that preventive medicine lacks drama or urgency. Yes, if you stop smoking you probably won't develop lung cancer thirty years from now. Maintain your normal weight and you'll be healthier in future decades. Control your tendency toward high blood pressure and you'll add years to the end of your life. Truisms, but dull, long-range and difficult to remember or apply on a day-to-day basis. In contrast, understanding and managing life change is significantly more urgent than counting calories or resisting tobacco as a preventive medical tool. Improperly handling life change can have its negative effects on your health tomorrow.

THE MOTHER-IN-LAW LINK

Harold G. Wolff began studies of illness onset in the 1930s at Cornell University Medical College and New York Hospital. In these pioneering years he found convincing evidence that common, everyday events helped cause a host of diseases, including many never previously considered "psychosomatic," for example, colds, skin diseases, and tuberculosis. In interviews with thousands of patients, Wolff and his colleagues, among them Thomas H. Holmes, learned that visits by mother-in-law were a major precipitant of common colds. Very seriously they concluded that the mother-in-law is a common health problem in North America.

In a continuation of these studies, Dr. Holmes and other researchers interviewed many hundreds of tuberculosis patients between 1949 and 1964. In virtually every case examined, the researchers found that victims of tuberculosis had experienced increasing life change before becoming ill; such events as jail terms, financial problems, marital separations, job changes, changes in residence, and personal injury. The researchers began to recognize a group of life changes that were repeatedly a prelude to disease. Not all of these life events were negative. Outstanding personal achievements, vacations, and the births of children also appeared significant, along with many ordinary events of life—mortgages, switching jobs, changing residences, and changes in financial situation. In time, these observations led to a scientific collaboration between Dr. Holmes, now at the University of Washington Medical School, and Dr. Richard H. Rahe, a neuropsychiatric researcher with the U. S. Navy.

Holmes, Rahe, and their colleagues assembled a list of life change events that had evolved from the tuberculosis studies and asked thousands of men and women in every imaginable walk of life to judge and rank the impact of the events. Obviously, the death of a parent ranked higher than a traffic ticket. But how did changing residences compare with taking a vacation? In the United States, Japan, and other countries, people were asked to make such decisions.

Incredibly, in all countries and regardless of age, income, occupation, sex, education, or religion, there was widespread agreement among people as to which life change events were most important and which were relatively minor. In turn, this data gave Holmes and Rahe the information required to assign numerical scores for each of the life change events, and then to conduct a second study to determine what, if any, influence accumulative life change might have on an individual's health.

In a research project of enormous scale, Holmes, Rahe, and their colleagues began compiling life-change scores and medical histories for thousands of people. ". . . seldom," Alvin Toffler wrote of this research in *Future Shock,* "were results of an experiment less ambiguous. In the United States and Japan, among servicemen and civilians, among pregnant women and the families of leukemia victims, among college athletes and retirees, the same striking pattern was present: those with high life-change scores were more likely than their fellows to be ill in the following year."

Holmes and Rahe were astonished at the results of their study, even a bit intimidated by them . . . they didn't publish their findings for five years!

Since 1967, when Holmes and Rahe finally released the Social Readjustment Rating Scale, or Life Change Scale, it has been retested with thousands of subjects in the United States, Japan, Belgium, the Netherlands, and France. The results are always the same. *Too much life change over a short period of time initiates illness, and the greater the amount of life change the more serious the illness.*

THE SOCIAL READJUSTMENT RATING SCALE
(Life Change Scale)

	Life Event	Mean Value
1.	Death of spouse	100
2.	Divorce	73
3.	Marital separation	65
4.	Jail term	63
5.	Death of close family member	63
6.	Personal injury or illness	53
7.	Marriage	50
8.	Fired at work	47

9.	Marital reconciliation	45
10.	Retirement	45
11.	Change in health of family member	44
12.	Pregnancy	40
13.	Sex difficulties	39
14.	Gain of new family member (a birth, adoption, oldster moving in)	39
15.	Business readjustment (e.g., merger, reorganization, bankruptcy)	39
16.	Change in financial state (a lot worse off or a lot better off than usual)	38
17.	Death of close friend	37
18.	Change to different line of work	36
19.	Change in number of arguments with spouse (either a lot more or a lot less than usual regarding child rearing, personal habits)	35
20.	Mortgage over $10,000 (e.g., purchasing a home, business)	31
21.	Foreclosure of mortgage or loan	30
22.	Change in responsibilities at work (promotion, demotion, or lateral transfer)	29
23.	Son or daughter leaving home (e.g., marriage, attending college)	29
24.	Trouble with in-laws	29
25.	Outstanding personal achievement	28
26.	Wife begin or stop work	26
27.	Begin or end school	26
28.	Change in living conditions (e.g., building a new house, remodeling, deterioration of home or neighborhood)	25
29.	Revision of personal habits (dress, manners, associations, etc.)	24
30.	Trouble with boss	23
31.	Change in work hours or conditions	20
32.	Change in residence	20
33.	Change in schools	20
34.	Change in recreation	19
35.	Change in church activities	19
36.	Change in social activities (e.g., clubs, dancing, movies, visiting)	18
37.	Mortgage or loan less than $10,000 (e.g., purchasing a car, TV, freezer)	17
38.	Change in sleeping habits (a lot more or a lot less sleep, or change in part of day when asleep)	16
39.	Change in number of family get-togethers	15

40. Change in eating habits (a lot more or a lot less food intake, or very different meal hours or surroundings) 15
41. Vacation 13
42. Christmas 12
43. Minor violations of the law (e.g., traffic ticket, jaywalking, disturbing the peace) 11

In using this scale, be sure to factor in the number of times you have experienced each of the life events during the past two years. For example, if you have changed residences three times in two years, you have accumulated 60 points (3 × 20) for that life event. If you have taken two vacations, you have accumulated 26 points (2 × 13) for the event. (In Dr. Holmes' laboratory a specialized test called the Schedule of Recent Experience is used to compile and quantify these variables. This Schedule of Recent Experience must be used in the statistical analysis of life change for the data to have scientific relevance. However, the Social Readjustment Rating Scale is perfectly suited for managing personal life change.)

Above all, remember that life changes are not necessarily bad, nor should all life changes be avoided. You can't escape many life changes, nor would you want to escape them. Vacations, job promotions, earning more money, births, retirement, and outstanding personal achievements are goals most of us value and strive for. The key is to pace yourself.

The higher your life-change score within a period of twenty-four months, the more likely you are to get sick. As we've mentioned earlier, among people with over 450 life-change units within the past two years, about 90 per cent will become ill in the near future. With 300 units the illness rate will drop to 66 per cent. Only about 33 per cent with 150 units will become ill. Obviously then, the higher your present score the more cautious you should be about tackling more life change. This is important, for it influences not only whether or not you may become ill but also how serious your illness may be. In other words, you may not be able to avoid the 200 units that precipitate your cold, but should you let your life-change units reach, say 500 or 600, instead of a minor cold you may develop a stomach ulcer, experience a heart attack, or have a serious automobile accident.

In addition to events listed on the Life Change Scale, be aware of life changes that are unusual to you because of your profession, life-style, or other circumstances. For example, in a study involving college athletes, troubles with the coach was ranked at 35 life-change units; being dropped from the team was assigned 52 life-change units. In any situation you recognize as stressful, you can assign a life-change score to the event by comparing it to the events on the Life Change Scale. Thus if you consider a situation more stressful than Christmas (12 units) but less stressful than changing residences (20 units), you can determine it has a life-change value of about 16.

SPECIALIZED LIFE-CHANGE SCALES

As scientists study the connection between life changes and illness, some remarkable new information is coming to light, and soon this data will lead to special life-change scales for particular groups within our population. Some of the most striking work in this area has been done by Dr. R. Dean Coddington, a professor of psychiatry and pediatrics at the Ohio State University College of Medicine. Dr. Coddington has pioneered life-change scales for children of various ages, and his results provide some insights into child development. Drawing the first few items from four different life-change scales, consider the most highly scored life-change events for preschool children, elementary school children, junior high children, and senior high adolescents.

PRESCHOOL AGE GROUP

	Life event	Life-change units
1.	Death of a parent	89
2.	Divorce of parents	78
3.	Marital separation of parents	74
4.	Jail sentence of parent for year or more	67
5.	Marriage of parent to stepparent	62

ELEMENTARY AGE GROUP

	Life event	Life-change units
1.	Death of a parent	91
2.	Divorce of parents	84
3.	Marital separation of parents	78
4.	Acquiring a physical deformity	69
5.	Death of a brother or sister	68

JUNIOR HIGH AGE GROUP

	Life event	Life-change units
1.	Unwed pregnancy	95
2.	Death of a parent	94
3.	Divorce of parents	84
4.	Acquiring a physical deformity	83
5.	Marital separation of parents	77
6.	Fathering an unwed pregnancy	76

SENIOR HIGH AGE GROUP

	Life event	Life-change units
1.	Getting married	101
2.	Unwed pregnancy	92
3.	Death of a parent	87
4.	Acquiring a physical deformity	81
5.	Divorce of parents	77
6.	Fathering an unwed pregnancy	77

In these studies Dr. Coddington found no social, class, or racial differences between the groups of children in terms of how they react to life changes. But not surprisingly, one can see how the significance of various life-change events for children change as they grow older. To the elementary school student pregnancy is of no concern whatsoever. To the high school student it is as significant as the loss of a parent.

As this work continues, specialized social readjustment rating scales are going to make great contributions to preventive medicine as rankings are developed for athletes, military personnel, college students, and children. In each of these categories research is well under way . . . it's only a beginning.

SERIOUSNESS OF ILLNESS

In 1971, Allen R. Wyler, Minoru Masuda, and Thomas H. Holmes published still another subtle bombshell related to Life Change, a paper titled "Magnitude of Life Events and Seriousness of Illness." In earlier studies these same researchers had created a Seriousness of Illness Scale, a list of 126 illnesses that had been ranked by both physicians and laymen as to how "serious" they felt the illnesses to be. Peptic ulcers were assigned a value of 500. Then the test participants were asked to rate other illnesses against ulcers in terms of such factors as prognosis, duration, threat to life, degree of disability, and degree of discomfort. Thus such woes as hiccups, constipation, shark bite, and sexual problems were compared to such recognized diseases as kidney infection, syphilis, and cancer. This is not as odd as it may seem, since by definition disease is any departure from health. Originally the word was a euphemism–*dis-ease,* not at ease. Although in popular usage the term is usually reserved for "traditional" illnesses, in fact a cut finger is a disease. Injuries sustained in an automobile accident represent disease, and the accident itself is part of the disease process.

When all the data was in, the combined rankings (least serious to most serious) looked like this:

Rank	Disease	SIU*
1.	Dandruff	21
2.	Warts	32
3.	Coldsore, canker sore	43
4.	Corns	46

* Seriousness of Illness Units

Rank	Disease	SIU
5.	Hiccups	48
6.	Bad breath	49
7.	Sty	59
8.	Common cold	62
9.	Farsightedness	72
10.	Nosebleed	73
11.	Sore throat	74
12.	Nearsightedness	75
13.	Sunburn	80
14.	Constipation	81
15.	Astigmatism	83
16.	Laryngitis	84
17.	Ringworm	85
18.	Headache	88
19.	Scabies	89
20.	Boils	96
21.	Heartburn	98
22.	Acne	103
23.	Abscessed tooth	108
24.	Color blindness	109
25.	Tonsillitis	117
26.	Diarrhea	118
27.	Carbuncle	122
28.	Chicken pox	134
29.	Menopause	140
30.	Mumps	148
31.	Dizziness	149
32.	Sinus infection	150
33.	Bedsores	153
34.	Increased menstrual flow	154
35.	Fainting	155
36.	Measles	159
37.	Painful menstruation	163
38.	Infection of the middle ear	164
39.	Varicose veins	173
40.	Psoriasis	174
41.	No menstrual period	175
42.	Hemorrhoids	177
43.	Hay fever	185
44.	Low blood pressure	189
45.	Eczema	204
46.	Drug allergy	206
47.	Bronchitis	210
48.	Hyperventilation	211
49.	Shingles	212

Rank	Disease	SIU
50.	Mononucleosis	216
51.	Infected eye	220
52.	Bursitis	222
53.	Whooping cough	230
54.	Lumbago	231
55.	Fibroids of the uterus	234
56.	Migraine	242
57.	Hernia	244
58.	Frostbite	263
59.	Goiter	283
60.	Abortion	284
61.	Ovarian cyst	288
62.	Heat stroke	293
63.	Gonorrhea	296
64.	Irregular heartbeats	302
65.	Overweight	309
66.	Anemia	312
67.	Anxiety reaction	315
68.	Gout	322
69.	Snake bite	324
70.	Appendicitis	337
71.	Pneumonia	338
72.	Depression	344
73.	Frigidity	347
74.	Burns	348
75.	Kidney infection	374
76.	Inability for sexual intercourse	382
77.	Hyperthyroidism	393
78.	Asthma	413
79.	Glaucoma	426
80.	Sexual deviation	446
81.	Gallstones	454
82.	Arthritis	468
83.	Starvation	473
84.	Syphilis	474
85.	Accidental poisoning	480
86.	Slipped disk	487
87.	Hepatitis	488
88.	Kidney stones	499
89.	Peptic ulcer	500
90.	Pancreatitis	514
91.	High blood pressure	520
92.	Smallpox	530
93.	Deafness	533

Rank	Disease	SIU
94.	Collapsed lung	536
95.	Shark bite	545
96.	Epilepsy	582
97.	Chest pain	609
98.	Nervous breakdown	610
99.	Diabetes	621
100.	Blood clot in vessels	631
101.	Hardening of the arteries	635
102.	Emphysema	636
103.	Tuberculosis	645
104.	Alcoholism	688
105.	Drug addiction	722
106.	Coma	725
107.	Cirrhosis of the liver	733
108.	Parkinson's disease	734
109.	Blindness	737
110.	Mental retardation	745
111.	Blood clot in the lung	753
112.	Manic depressive psychosis	766
113.	Stroke	774
114.	Schizophrenia	785
115.	Muscular dystrophy	785
116.	Congenital heart defects	794
117.	Tumor in spinal cord	800
118.	Cerebral palsy	805
119.	Heart failure	824
120.	Heart attack	855
121.	Brain infection	872
122.	Multiple sclerosis	875
123.	Bleeding in brain	913
124.	Uremia	963
125.	Cancer	1020
126.	Leukemia	1080

Using this instrument, the researchers investigated the amount of life-change experience by 232 randomly selected patients who, as it turned out, collectively suffered forty-two different kinds of disease. The results of this study again spotlighted life change as a prelude to illness, but the stunning new development was a correlation between the quantity of life change and the seriousness of illness as ranked on the Seriousness of Illness Rating Scale. In other words, the greater the amount of life change the worse the illness. Here is a sampling of the more dramatic data from this study:

Illness	(Seriousness of illness units in parentheses)	Number of patients	Mean average life change units in the 2 years preceding the illness
Headache	(88)	5	209
Acne	(103)	6	311
Psoriasis	(174)	6	317
Eczema	(204)	7	231
Bronchitis	(210)	8	322
Hernia	(244)	9	457
Anemia	(312)	7	325
Anxiety reaction	(315)	4	482
Gallstones	(454)	6	563
Peptic ulcer	(500)	17	603
High blood pressure	(520)	4	405
Chest pain	(609)	7	638
Diabetes	(621)	6	599
Alcoholism	(688)	3	688
Manic-depressive psychosis	(766)	4	753
Schizophrenia	(785)	12	609
Heart failure	(824)	9	772
Cancer	(1020)	15	777

To be sure, not all the results were so dramatic as these, but from a scientist's point of view the research project was a leap forward in understanding the connection between life change and the seriousness of resulting illness. The figures showed that patients with greatest life-change unit scores were more likely to suffer a serious illness, and frequently these were serious chronic illnesses. Patients with lower scores were more apt to have minor illnesses, and they were more likely to be acute.[1]

[1] Chronic illnesses are those that don't go away quickly or become progressively worse in time. Acute illnesses are those with short courses. They may be very severe, but normally respond to a specific treatment.

USING THE LIFE CHANGE SCALE

Here we have an invaluable aid for maintaining better health, an instrument global in nature and simple to use. The following are suggestions for using the Life Change Scale on a day-by-day basis:

1. Become familiar with the life-change events.
2. Put the scale where you and your family can see it several times a day, perhaps on a kitchen bulletin board or inside a bathroom cabinet.
3. Evaluate how you feel when a life-change event occurs.
4. Think about the meaning of life-change events as they occur, and think about ways you might best adapt to these events.
5. Take your time in arriving at decisions.
6. When possible, anticipate life changes and plan for them well in advance.
7. Pace yourself. It can be done even if you are in a hurry.
8. Look at the accomplishment of a task as a part of daily living and avoid looking at such an achievement as a "stopping point" or a time for "letting down."[2]

Conscientiously employed, the Life Change Scale is the most valuable preventive medical tool available to us at the present time, and it should be incorporated into every physical examination.

The scale could be a constructive aid to thoughtful personnel management as well. The practice may be shy of ethical, but some corporations use physical examinations in the assessment of employees' qualifications for advancement. Presumedly the screening of an employee's past and recent health history is in the best interests of the corporations that follow

[2] Why this point is so critical to health is explained in Chapter 7.

this policy. It would be in an employee's best interest if an examination were made of his current life-change-unit accumulation prior to any decision involving an assignment change, promotion, or geographical transfer. This practice would greatly benefit employees, and it would also reduce absenteeism, increase productivity, lower group insurance rates, and reduce personnel problems in general; it would constructively serve *both* the company and employee.

Likewise, our military hierarchy could accomplish much to reduce diseases and accidents among military personnel by giving serious study to the impact of life change. For hundreds of thousands of men and women in the armed forces, the Pentagon wields awesome control over who will become sick and who will stay well merely through everyday decisions involving promotions, transfers, changes in living quarters, work assignments, menus, and training procedures. There are far more military casualties resulting from inattention to the devastating effects of life change than from bullets, missiles, or bombs.

HELPING OTHERS

Hal and Martha, presented in Chapter 1, typify the problems associated with too much life change. Both fell victim to popular ideas of how to cope with problems. In the case of Martha, divorced in New York, her reaction was to "start over again" on the West Coast. After the death of his wife, Hal's daughter convinced him to leave his woes behind and move to another city. Far better had both of them utilized the foregoing suggestions for managing life change.

All of us have witnessed the tragedy of someone dying suddenly just weeks after burying his spouse, or the accident-proneness of someone recently divorced, or a life that seems to come unraveled in the wake of mishap heaped upon mishap. Often, if not always, such unhappy people receive counsel from friends and relatives that is well intentioned but disastrous. Do not always assume that "leaving that old house with its sad memories" is the best course of action for someone bereaved, or that "remaking a life" is best for someone whose present life-style has been interrupted. True, in urging your elderly parent to stay in the old homestead you may incur the ire of other family members, but you may also keep that beloved parent around for a few years longer.

Life changes are insidious, and we initiate most of them ourselves. As the cartoon-hero Pogo said, "We have met the enemy, and he is us."

CHAPTER 6

COPING BEHAVIORS

Despite the awesome body of data substantiating a relationship between life change, stress, and illness, the statistics raise a nagging question. What about the healthy minority, the approximate 10 per cent who do not become ill or suffer accidents even when they have accumulated high scores on the life-change scale within short periods of time? And what about the 33 per cent with over 300 points who don't get sick? The answer is at once simple and complex–*coping behaviors.* The essential explanation for why life change induces illness is that life change requires one to adapt to or cope with a stressful life event. A few individuals display a near fathomless ability to muster coping behaviors, or coping mechanisms, to deal with life changes; these people never get sick. A few people rely on only one or two coping behaviors and are sick all the time. Most of us fall somewhere between in the number of coping behaviors we utilize.

Coping behaviors include emotional responses (anger, sorrow, elation), personal habits (eating, smoking, physical activity, sex), unconscious habits (nail biting, sighing, finger drumming). Attention to one's job and hobbies are coping behaviors, as is time spent with one's family. Coping behaviors may be harmful especially if just one or two are relied upon. If eating becomes a primary coping behavior, obesity is the likely result. In our culture the use of alcohol and other drugs as coping mechanisms has created a problem epidemic in scope.

In an illustration less dramatic than drug abuse, consider someone whose primary coping behavior is anger. This is a person who doesn't know how to compromise, retreat, intellectualize, or laugh. Yet at an absolute minimum such an individual, like everyone else, faces 100 or so situations a year that require some kind of reaction. Being stopped by a policeman for speeding, for example, or being delayed in traffic, or perhaps being told the dry cleaning has not come back on time. The angry person's reaction is always the same, even when anger is not an appropriate or advantageous reaction. As a result, the angry person is often in trouble and finds it impossible to deal with life. Such a person cannot hold a job for long, maintain close personal relationships, or function socially. As patients, such individuals are never satisfied with their doctors; as students they rebel against their teachers; as employees they are infuriated by their bosses. Everything and everybody makes them mad. In similar patterns, there are people who only know how to get depressed, or only know how to withdraw.

People who get along fairly well in life are those who can respond to any given situation with perhaps a dozen or more different coping behaviors. They know different responses to a given stimulus. They can react with anger, sorrow, laughter, and logic. They know how to do whatever a given situation calls for. These are the people who can handle a considerable amount of life change.

WHEN ILLNESS IS YOUR COPING BEHAVIOR

Illness itself is often a coping behavior, and when illness occurs in someone who has a poverty of other coping behaviors to call upon, the illness usually becomes a dominant behavior. Such patients may never get well. In the study of open-heart surgery patients described at the end of Chapter 3, the Group II patients, or symbiotic group, "were achieving gains being sick." They really didn't know how to be well or what to do if they were well. This was a group of patients who had embraced heart disease as their major coping behavior, and of the fifteen patients only one was improved by surgery.

Obviously, this is a complicated area of human behavior, and it is at last receiving some scientific attention. The most widely celebrated work in this field has been Friedman and Rosenman's studies of heart disease, popularized in their book *Type A Behavior and Your Heart*. Type A personalities develop heart disease, say Friedman and Rosenman, while Type B personalities do not. Type A's are driven, aggressive, ambitious, competitive, anxious to get things done, racing with the clock. Type B's are more easygoing, less competitive, not preoccupied with achievement, and unconcerned about time.

When Friedman and Rosenman first announced their findings, the outraged rebuttals came from all directions. Behavior and heart disease? What about cholesterol? Smoking? Obesity? Inheritance? Such criticisms have diminished as numerous studies (some of them having been under way for the past twenty years) are announced that corroborate Friedman and Rosenman.

One dramatic illustration. For years it had been observed that Japanese men suffered far fewer heart attacks than American men, and it was concluded that the reason was diet. Men in Japan eat more fish than meat; their cholesterol intake is much lower than that of American males. This was a good theory (it's still popular), but the evidence keeps mounting to refute it. One example, of many, was announced in 1975, a ten-year study at the University of California at Berkeley that had monitored some four thousand Japanese-American men. Through a period of ten years their serum cholesterol levels were regularly checked and compared to levels in control groups in Hawaii and Japan. At the end of the ten years no significant difference was noted between average cholesterol levels in the California group and the control groups. The only major difference between the groups was that the Californians' heart-attack rate increased to match that of other men in America! The research concluded it was American working habits and job-related stress that increased the incidence of heart disease.[1]

While it only seems logical that obesity contributes to heart disease, contradictions do occur. Dr. Jean Mayer, a professor of nutrition at Harvard, points out that some centenarians are quite obese (and some smoke as well). In any event, it is probable that heart disease is to some extent inherited, but perhaps not genetically as is widely claimed. "It is well within the realm of possibility," say Friedman and Rosenman, "that only too often they (heart disease patients) inherit from one or both of their parents a specific type of personality, one that may give rise to a behavior pattern . . . . which in turn leads to diseased coronary arteries." In other words, it may not be a physical predisposition toward disease the heart patient inherits from parents, but a destructive pattern of behaviors. Work of this sort is turning medical thinking around as more data accumulates linking cancer, heart disease, and a majority of other major illnesses to behavior and attitude.

The following "verbal statements of attitudes" hardly represent a comprehensive review of current work in the field, but these simple statements are drawn from a considerable body of clinical experience. They may not seem to correspond with your attitude or point of view when you have one of these illnesses. However, in many instances they provide insight into specific diseases as coping behaviors, and they can be valuable. For example, if you have high blood pressure and you sense that you do feel a need to be on guard and alert, con-

[1] Japanese corporations tend to establish a paternal relationship with their employees. Employees are seldom fired and there is little direct competition between them.

sider changing your point of view. If successful in altering your reaction to stressful events, it may lower your blood pressure.

VERBAL STATEMENTS OF ATTITUDES IN ASSOCIATION WITH ILLNESSES[2]

Acne. This person feels picked upon or picked at, and wants to be left alone. He feels nagged at.

Asthma. This person feels left out in the cold and wants to shut another person or situation out. He feels unloved, rejected, disapproved of, shut out, and wishes he didn't have to deal with the other person or situation. He would like to blot the person or situation out; not to have anything to do with the person or situation.

Backache. This person wants to run away, to get out, to walk right out of there, to escape.

Constipation. This person feels in a situation from which nothing good will come, yet keeps on with it grimly. He feels things will never get any better, but has to stick with it.

Diabetes. This person is starving in the midst of plenty. He is surrounded by most of the things that have meaning, but his perception is that none is available to him.

Diarrhea. This person sees himself faced with a meaningful task and wishes it were over, finished, or done with. He wishes the impending event were behind him.

[2] In the main, these are the clinical and teaching observations of David T. Graham, William J. Grace, and Thomas H. Holmes.

The experimental evidence behind these statements is fascinating. Under hypnosis, patients with histories of and/or predispositions toward these diseases can be coaxed into attacks or symptoms merely by suggesting the attitudes to them, or reminding them of the attitudes. For example, an asthma patient, when told he feels unloved, rejected, or shut out—while under hypnosis—will experience an asthma attack. What's more, even people in "perfect health" sometimes respond. Under hypnosis, someone with normal blood pressure, when told to be on guard, alert to danger, and ready for anything, will experience a modest elevation in blood pressure.

Duodenal Ulcer. This is a patient who feels deprived of what is due him, and he wants to get even. He does not get what he should, is owed, or is promised. He wants to do to some other person what that person has done to him.

Eczema (an itching and redness of the skin). This person feels he is being frustrated and can do nothing about it. He feels interfered with, blocked, prevented from doing something; he feels unable to make himself understood.

Heartburn. This person is getting what he wants.

Hernia. This person feels like exploding. His focus of attention is on controlling feelings of anger rather than the object of the anger.

Hives. This person feels he is taking a beating and is helpless to do anything about it. He is being knocked around, hammered on, being mistreated or unfairly treated.

Hyperthyroidism. This person feels he might lose somebody or something he loves and takes care of, and is trying to prevent the loss of the loved person or object. He is trying to hold on to somebody loved and taken care of who is being taken away.

Hypertension (high blood pressure). This person feels threatened with harm and has to be ready for something. He feels in danger; anything could happen at any time from any side; he has to be prepared to meet all possible threats; he has to be on guard. Typically, the executive who refuses to attend any meeting without an advance briefing will have a predisposition toward high blood pressure.

Metabolic Edema (fluid in tissues). This person feels he is carrying a heavy load and wants somebody else to carry all or part of it. He has too much on his shoulders, too much responsibility; he wants others to take their share of it.

Migraine. This person feels something has been achieved and then relaxes after the effort. He has to accomplish something, is driving himself, striving. He has to get things done. A goal must be reached. Then he lets down and stops the driving.

Multiple Sclerosis. This person feels forced to undertake some kind of physical activity, but he wants not to. He has to work without help, has to support himself and usually others. He wants not to, and wishes help or support.

Nausea and Vomiting. This person feels something wrong has happened for which he feels responsible. He is sorry it happened, and he wishes he could undo it. He wishes things were the way they were before. He wishes he had not done it.

Paroxysmal Auricular Tachycardia (irregular heart function). This person feels that things are not proceeding according to schedule and that they should be speeding up. Typical statements: "Let's get going. Let's get things started."

Psoriasis (a chronic recurrent skin disease). This person feels there is a constant gnawing at him, and that he has to put up with it. A steady boring, a constant nagging or irritation or annoyance is gnawing at him.

Raynaud's Disease (a nervous-system disturbance; a primary symptom can be painful cold hands). This person wants to take hostile physical action. She (the disease is most common among young women) wants to hit or strangle; she wants to take action of any kind. She has to do something.

Regional Enteritis (an inflammation of the small intestine). This person feels he has received something harmful and wants to get rid of it. He has been given or received something damaged or inferior; he feels he has been poisoned; he wants the situation to be finished, over, done with, disposed of.

Rheumatoid Arthritis. This person feels tied down and wants to get free. He feels restrained, restricted, confined, and he wants to move around.

Tuberculosis. Despite a valiant effort, this person feels overwhelmed by circumstances.

Ulcerative Colitis. This person feels he is being injured and degraded and wishes to get rid of the responsible agent. He is being humiliated; he wants the situation to be finished, over and done with, disposed of.

CHICKENS AND EGGS

Critics of attaching associations to diseases and attitudes point out that these kinds of observations are retrospective. It's quite natural, they like to say, that a psoriasis patient might feel a constant irritation because of the disease, or that a teen-ager with severe acne might well want to be left alone because of embarrassment over her skin condition. Here we have a classic chicken-and-egg analogy. Overriding evidence indicates that if the teen-ager's feelings of embarrassment can be diminished then the acne will go away. Yet keep in mind that *the attitude is not responsible for the disease; it is part of the disease process.*

Along similar paths, the medical community has debated for years as to whether such diseases as schizophrenia were the result of "physical" or "mental" causes. Experimental evidence can be mustered to indicate both, according to a majority of textbooks. In fact, the evidence demonstrates that the "physical" and "mental" signs of schizophrenia are inexorably related.

Outside the discipline of psychophysiology, some younger doctors have a difficult time perceiving illnesses and coping behaviors as being related, largely because of the way in which our medical schools view diseases; isolated acute disorders with specific causes. In contrast, older doctors who have had considerable experience with a great many patients often develop insight into the real nature of illness. Exploring this volatile subject with an eminent orthopedic surgeon, a physician with thirty years of acclaimed clinical experience behind him, we frankly expected a quarrel. What, after all, might seem less psychiatric than broken bones and their repair? The doctor's response to the suggestion that most illnesses, including bone fractures, are psychiatric in origin was, "I know that. Anyone who has been in medical practice as long as I have knows that." This was no isolated or maverick comment. It reflected what our very best doctors ponder when they confide in each other.

MEASURING YOUR COPING BEHAVIORS

In the 1950s Dr. Beatrice B. Berle found a direct correlation between *psychosocial assets* and coping ability. This makes logical sense, because the greater one's coping ability the better one will get along socially, and vice versa. The following is an adaptation of Berle's test, a quick and easy instrument with which you can obtain a rough measurement of your coping abilities. That is, the approximate number of coping behaviors you might have available in order to adjust to a given life change. Approached seriously, this can be a helpful and informative exercise.

COPING SCALE
DIRECTIONS

For each question, check a box indicating *Yes* or *No* to the question. Give a *Yes* or *No* if at all possible. If you feel that you do not know the answer, or if it is one half *Yes* and one half *No,* check both *Yes* and *No.*

There are no right or wrong answers, and a "high" score is not necessarily better than a "low" score and a "low" score is not necessarily better than a "high" score.

PART A

	YES	NO
1. Do people who know you well think you get upset easily?		

	YES	NO
2. Do people who know you well think you are stubborn?		
3. Do people who know you well think you understand other people's points of view and accept them the way they are?		
4. Do people who know you well think that when you get mad you get over it quickly?		
5. Do people who know you well think you overcome problems easily?		
6. Do people who know you well think you are reliable and responsible in meeting your financial obligations?		
7. Do people who know you well think you have continued to mature and grow emotionally as you have gotten older?		
8. Do you think the way you adjust to life can contribute to getting sick?		
9. Do you think that changing your life in some way might make it easier to get well once you get sick?		
10. If you were sick and were told to treat yourself with something that you did not understand and was difficult, but which no one would know about if you did not do it, would you do it?		

PART B

	YES	NO
1. Do you have good health?		
2. Do you think you had a satisfying religious education?		
3. Do you think your father was supportive and understanding?		
4. Do you think your mother was supportive and understanding?		
5. Do you think those close to you provide the emotional support you need?		
6. Do you think your housing is a problem?		
7. Are you satisfied with your occupation?		
8. Are you satisfied with your working condition?		
9. Is your income satisfactory?		
10. Have you set goals for the future that satisfy you and are realistic?		

To score the test, give yourself five points for every *Yes* item in Part A *except* items 1 and 2. For these give yourself five points for *No* answers.

Give yourself five points for every *Yes* answer in Part B *except* item 6. For this item give yourself five points for a *No* answer.

Wherever you answer the opposite of above, give yourself negative five points. Where you've answered *Yes* and *No* to an item you receive zero points. Thus it is possible to score between −100 and +100 combining the scores from Parts A and B.

If you score over 80 on this test you have excellent coping abilities; you may even be among the 10 per cent to 20 per cent of our society who never get sick (but don't try your luck!).

If you score below 40 on this test, you are shy in coping ability.

If you approach a negative score on the test, the probability that you can adapt to more life change is very poor. Should you become sick, the illness itself might become your major coping behavior and you could have a difficult time improving.

Scores between 40 and 80 are less reliable than scores higher or lower. In this range you should manage your life-change units with caution. Most of us fall into this category.

HOW TO COPE WHEN YOU CAN'T

Anyone operating with a minimum of coping behaviors is usually obvious. Extreme obesity, alcoholism, or a complete inability to get along with people are examples, but there are myriad others. Such situations are difficult, *but by no means hopeless.*

Coping behaviors are basically responses learned either by observation or experience. Thus new coping behaviors can be acquired by 1) finding a professional who is knowledgeable enough and tolerant enough to help you; and 2) learning to employ that person's coping behaviors.

The professional might be a well-educated minister, an understanding employer, a well-trained social worker, a physician. The key is that this person understand your problem and, in a sense, put up with it. In return, you should study and try to affect as many of this person's coping behaviors as you can.

If the mere exercise of imitating someone else's coping behaviors strikes you as an overly simple solution to your coping difficulties, consider how most of us, in fact virtually all of us, develop through childhood and adolescence into adulthood. We learn by imitation. To alter, revise, or reverse attitudes seeded in youth, new role models are necessary.

Imagine you are the angry person described earlier, the man or woman who can deal only with travail, confrontations, or even minor difficulties by overreacting. Among the people you flare up at, your boss may well head the list. If he is still your boss after several such episodes, you have an excellent opportunity to expand your capacity for coping. When you explode in anger at your employer, notice how he deals with the situation (assuming he understands your problem and behaves rationally himself). Why can't you try to react to job pressure the way he does instead of becoming angry? This is not easy, to be sure, but it can be accomplished, and it's very worth-while.

Essentially, this is how Alcoholics Anonymous functions. Members teach new members new coping behaviors (by example) to replace old, destructive behaviors.

To learn new coping behaviors, select a tolerant and informed professional to mimic. It's also helpful to remember that effectively coping is wholly unrelated to performance or perfection in any given situation. Coping has nothing to do with achievement, making the team, capturing a lover, or being envied by others. An openness to receiving help from others may be a more valid coping strategy than trying to do everything yourself. Being able to cry, to ask questions, to take time for orientation or preparation, to delay taking action—all of these are appropriate ways of dealing with life change and with stress.

CHAPTER 7

THE COLTER COASTER

Remember John Colter's adventure, described in Chapter 2? He generated enormous amounts of energy to maintain his physical activation while escaping the Blackfoot Indians. But later on that tumultuous day, while hiding in a log jam over the Jefferson River, John conserved energy. While he was thus concealed, his withdrawal allowed him to save remaining energy, and to replenish supplies of energy for his eventual long trek back to Fort Lisa and safety. Most of us lead lives marked by naturally occurring cycles of activation and withdrawal, not so dramatic perhaps as John Colter's on the day he escaped the Indians, but physiologically similar nevertheless. In some of us, this naturally occurring cycling is symptomatic of disease. When activation and withdrawal are somewhat similar to what Colter experienced, on a biorhythmic basis, the condition is called manic-depressive disease, a psychiatric illness. Diseases associated with lesser degrees of activation-withdrawal cycling are asthma, emphysema, heart attacks, strokes, diabetes mellitus, migraine headaches, tension headaches, backaches, high blood pressure, duodenal ulcers, and schizophrenia . . . to mention only a few. The combination of any of these illnesses with manic-depressive disease is usually disastrous.

Normally it doesn't matter whether activation is vigorous exercise, anger, anxiety, euphoria, or excitement. It is the activation, or *action orientation,* rather than the specific activity or emotion that precipitates some illness symptoms. The same holds true for withdrawal. It usually doesn't matter if withdrawal is due to sleep, depression, apathy, or a conditioned inhibition of activity. It is the withdrawal, or *non-action orientation,* that triggers certain disease symptoms. (Since Transcendental Meditation and Relaxation Response are conditioned inhibitions of activity, they can, under some circumstances, make you sick.)

Often a disease which seems hopeless and impossible to control is simply a response to rapidly occurring changes in activation. Such a disease may suddenly come under control, or even go away, when the cycling of activation is stopped. It wasn't until physiologists began to study psychiatry and psychiatrists began to study physiology that this extraordinary insight into disease came to light. But the past few years have seen considerable exploration into this facet of medicine, and the upshot is a calculable link between a great many diseases and swings in activation-withdrawal behavior. Many such diseases can be placed on a simple graph that, having no official name yet, might as well be labeled the Colter Coaster.

THE RELAXATION TRAP

We've become so preoccupied with relaxation and peace of mind in recent years that we have neglected relaxation's association with diseases and disease symptoms.

Yes, relaxation may be dangerous to your health. As indicated by the coastering illustration, some diseases and disease symptoms are associated with relaxation, or non-action orientation. These diseases can be every bit as distressing as those associated with action orientation.

minishes, the first symptom may be spots before the eyes, followed by nausea, vomiting, abdominal distress, weakness in an arm or leg, and even weakness of one side of the body.

One such patient was a successful thirty-five-year-old surgeon who came in for treatment because he was convinced that he was going insane. This was a talented, hard-driving doctor who normally put in long hours. He seemed to thrive on work. It was at home, frequently after a cocktail, that his migraine headaches appeared. Often they occurred on weekends and holidays. Finally he consulted with a friend, another physician, who told him he was working too hard and that he'd have to relax more. So he eased up, relaxed more, and his headaches got worse. He was told he still wasn't relaxing enough, so he tried meditation and drugs to help him relax. And the more he meditated and the more he relaxed the more frequent and severe the headaches were. He began to think he was going insane and that the pain was "all in my mind."

When at last he began to see the relationship between his headaches and his activity level, he took the following steps: He decreased his level of activation during the day by maintaining his normal working hours but decreasing his case load, and he increased his level of activation in the afternoon and evening by doing paperwork. He mainly saw patients in the morning, worked on papers in the afternoon and read journals in the evening. After several weeks of taking some of his work home, and thinking about work at home, he was headache free. To avoid the headaches he simply decreased the intensity of swings in activation. He flattened out his Colter Coaster. Once he established the changed pattern, his briefcase began to symbolize work, and thinking about it was sufficient to maintain a high enough activity level during evenings and weekends to avoid triggering headaches.

What is the explanation for this? The migraine headache is very real, physiologically. It occurs when there is a contraction followed by a relaxation of any cranial artery with an accumulation of fluid in the tissue around the arterial wall. The pressure of blood in the artery distends the artery wall and produces pain. Since this can happen to any artery in the head, the pain can occur anywhere. Classically, however, it appears as a one-sided, throbbing headache.

The aura which usually precedes a migraine headache (spots before the eyes, muscular weakness, dizziness, flashes of light) is due to a constriction of the artery to the point that the blood supply is diminished and therefore the oxygen level is insufficient to support the tissues the artery supplies. The tissue in this case is usually nerve tissue in the brain. Since this can occur in any artery of the head, just about any symptom is possible, and it can be devastating. If the reduction in blood flow occurs in the middle cerebral artery, for example, the patient will experience a paralysis of one side of the body. This is called migraine hemiplegia. More often, however, the arterial constriction weakens an arm or leg, or it may produce a short period in which the patient doesn't know where he or she is—*dissociation.*

People with the kind of activation pattern that produces migraine symptoms are frequently called *hysterical* or diagnosed as having a *conversion reaction,*[1] hoary old psychological terms that do the patient a disservice since they imply the symptoms are the patient's fault. In some circumstances appropriate care may even be denied. An illustration of this involved a medical intern training in a major medical school teaching hospital.

After working frightfully hard for several months of internship without any time off, the intern was rewarded with a vacation, recognition of his good work. He left work for home, at ease for perhaps the first time in over a year. His wife surprised him with a pitcher of martinis, and the two discussed plans for their vacation to another state. Then his wife exited to the kitchen to prepare a celebration dinner while he stretched out on the couch. A couple of hours later, when she called him for dinner, he was asleep. She went back to the

[1] Defined as the transformation of emotions into physical manifestations.

couch and shook him awake to discover he couldn't speak and his right side was paralyzed. He was taken by ambulance to the hospital where no cause for the symptoms could be found. The intern was diagnosed as having a conversion reaction and he was scoffed at by several of his colleagues. The paralysis cleared during the night and he awoke unattended with an unbearable, throbbing left-side headache.

If you suffer migraine headaches, or if you know anyone who does, you'll recognize a pattern similar to the two preceding case histories. The classic migraine appears in someone whose Colter Coaster is like that of, say, the wife of a traveling salesman. While he's on the road the wife is "in charge" of the household, active, tense, alert. Alone, she must discipline the children, cope with minor plumbing problems, put out the dog at night. When her husband returns home she is much relieved and she relaxes . . . and gets a throbbing migraine headache. After months or years of this, alas, the husband may begin to prefer being on the road to being home.

WHEN VACATIONS CAN BE KILLERS

Cerebrovascular accidents in the form of "strokes" (caused by a blood clot in an artery supplying blood to the brain) occur in settings similar to those in which migraines occur.

Strokes seem to occur in people who live pressured lives. They live this way because they want to, not in response to pressures from their peers or business obligations. They feel a need to keep busy, to project self-images as active hard workers. They want to maintain high standards, take on responsibilities. They thrive on a sense of urgency, need to fulfill goals. They are strong-willed and determined. To be sure, these are the kind of people we expect to suffer strokes, but contrary to popular notions, the strokes do not occur during the height of such pressured life-styles. A stroke is more likely to occur when such a life-style is terminated by something not under the patient's control. The patient feels a loss of control and interprets it as a personal failure.

The emotion most frequently experienced in the period preceding a stroke is anger, in association with hopelessness, helplessness, and an inability to correct the situation. The life events which initiate such a termination of life-style are usually personal feelings, environmental obstacles which block the patient's activation, loss of status as being useful or needed, loss of control over objects, real or threatened loss of an object, or the failure of others to meet the patient's standards.

A forest-industry executive who started with his company thirty years previously at age twenty-five and worked his way to an executive position responsible for a multimillion-dollar division provides an example of the stroke phenomenon. For thirty years he was highly motivated and activated, never letting down and always achieving his goals. He finally reached the very responsible position he had been aiming for, but now there was no place else to go. There were no promotions possible and he was helpless to do anything about it. His pressured life-style was no longer successful in getting him what he wanted, i.e., another rung up the ladder. There were no more rungs.

The executive interpreted this situation as a personal failure and began acting irrational. The company's board of directors discerned that a highly respected executive was having personal difficulties and interpreted them as being related to his many years of service and high-pressured pace. They gave him a six-month paid leave to the Caribbean. He left with his wife for a long, "well earned" rest and within two weeks suffered a stroke that paralyzed his right arm and leg. A well-intended, forced change in activity ended up a family, personal, and corporate disaster.

How did this happen? A man in the prime of his life had a stroke while he was doing something that he should enjoy. The actual mechanics are not certain; however, it's possible to make an educated guess.

In maintaining a pressured life-style, the heart is accustomed to pumping more blood at a higher pressure than average. The blood also clots faster. With a termination of the activation pattern, the blood pressure and total amount of blood flow diminish rapidly. With the reduction in pressure and flow, the blood moves more slowly through the blood vessels. This is significant, because a man at age fifty-five undoubtedly has some narrowing of the arteries in the brain. The rapid clotting of blood that is associated with activation does not necessarily slow down at the same rate as does the reduction in blood flow. Therefore, there is a period of maximum vulnerability when the blood clots rapidly, the cardiac output is low, and blood is moving sluggishly through vessels that are partially occluded. If a clot is going to form and block the flow of blood, these are the optimum conditions. An additional factor may be an arterial narrowing resulting from the initial migraine phenomenon, which could even further decrease blood flow.

Whatever the precise mechanisms that cause them, the strokes are terribly real, and they are brought on by sudden and wide fluctuations between action orientation and non-action orientation–coastering. In turn, the coaster is normally activated by too much life change. Once you get the coaster rolling you are at the mercy of your own biology and whatever coping behaviors you have learned in the past.

WHY BACKACHES OFTEN DON'T GO AWAY

Few symptoms confound both patients and doctors more often than back pain. Back-pain patients sometimes suffer for years while having no apparent physical reason to be in pain. The pain, however, is very real and uncomfortable. And it is related to activation.

Since the function of skeletal muscles is to move the body, tension of one's musculature is a requirement of motion and physical activity. Even thinking about physical action increases muscle activity, as do emotions. For example, anxiety, anger, and euphoria are conditions closely related to the expenditure of energy. Anxiety is an emotion we experience when we are prepared for action. Anger is an emotion we experience when the action is destructive. Euphoria is an emotion we experience when we "are on top of the world" and want to interact with and enjoy life.

Whatever the reason for activation, increased muscle activity results in an increase of blood flow to the muscles. However, when the muscle contraction is sustained there is a relative decrease in blood flow, an increased use of oxygen, and an accumulation of toxic wastes which produce pain. Essentially, this is why it hurts to hold a heavy object too long.

The same mechanism appears to produce many backaches in everyday life. That is, sustained muscle contraction in preparation for action occurring in the absence of action produces pain in the involved muscles. The neck and back muscles are the most frequently involved. If the contemplated action is actually carried out, pain is usually avoided, however, other types of problems may result. With the venting of anger the action may take the form of slugging your boss or hitting a brick wall with your fist. In the case of anxiety you may run away from responsibilities. Euphoria may lead to a day on the ski slopes or other pleasant diversions instead of going to work. Any of these actions may lead to trouble, but at least they'll prevent backache.

As a rule, muscle contractions do not occur without accompanying activating emotions. What's more, activating emotions normally do not occur without muscle tension, hence the crux of the problem for patients with back pain. A person who suffers a back injury may slip into this cycle and never get well.

When you hurt your back and the muscles are tense and painful from the injury, you may well want to take action to halt the pain. This emotional response will, in turn, increase your muscle tension and pain which will, in turn, increase your desire to take some constructive action. On a day-to-day basis such an association between activating emotions and muscle tension is both an asset and a liability. On the one hand this feedback prepares us for activity; on the other it can produce incapacitating symptoms.

It doesn't seem to matter what initiates the pain. The initial stimulus may be a physical back injury or activating emotions, but once the pain is established it may sustain itself by triggering a feedback which induces activating emotions, muscle tension, and more pain.

Ironically, people for whom back pain can be the most troublesome are the same ones most likely to develop back pain. Those of us who feel a need to be overactive (a popular coping behavior) are also the ones most likely to develop back pain.

BETWEEN A ROCK AND A HARD PLACE

A case history exemplifying the relationship between high activation and back pain is provided by a thirty-three-year-old nurse who experienced moderate to severe back pain for five years after a minor accident.

This was a woman who led a hectic social and professional life. She was a skilled rock climber, mountaineer, tennis player, and president of one of her professional groups. Her hyperactive life was interrupted, however, because of an insignificant fall during a rock-climbing outing in the Olympic Mountains of Washington. The fall initiated moderate pain in the lower back area. She and her companions agreed that the injury was inconvenient but minor, and she hiked some fifteen miles back to a roadhead the following day. Along the trail her back pain increased.

Safe and warm back home she was unable to "relax and take it easy." Her life-style demanded that she stay busy. Typical of people who suffer back pain, she felt the condition was one she could not afford to have, since proper care included avoiding situations that might reinjure her back. Indeed, she tried to maintain her usual pace of physical activity, subdued only in response to her physical pain. After several months of this she began to notice that each time she thought about a physical or mental activity her back became tense and the low level of pain she constantly experienced increased in intensity. She was convinced that the pain was still a result of her injury in the Olympics, and after enduring it for some six months she arranged for a medical consultation.

After a complete physical examination, including numerous laboratory tests, she was told that there was nothing wrong with her back. It was suggested that she treat her pain with medication and behavioral techniques designed to relax her. What her doctor could not know was that she couldn't tolerate relaxation and would not follow the prescribed treatment. She simply avoided the relaxation techniques; she either did not take the medication or took overdoses sufficient to put her asleep because she could not abide the feelings of lethargy it induced. In this setting her pain increased and within a year of her injury it was sufficient to drastically limit her activity.

Now she began to feel depressed and irritable, and the pain began to radiate down both her legs.

Again she sought medical consultation and was told it was possible that she had a ruptured intervertebral disk. However, a painful examination of her spinal cord proved inconclusive. Her physician felt she should not have surgery, but the decision was hers, and she knew she could not adhere to the treatment prescribed since she could not tolerate the reduction in her activity level. She decided to have the surgery, since to her any opportunity for a reduction of the pain was worth the price.

Surgery was performed, and the results, as expected, indicated she had a healthy, normal back. Nevertheless for three months following the operation she was free of pain and she was delighted!

On the fourth month following surgery she fell on a tennis

court while trying to return a fast serve. She immediately felt pain in her lower back. Thus commenced another six months of increasingly severe pain that initiated a drastic cutback in her activity level along with increasing depression and irritability. Again, her physician told her she had a normal and healthy back, and this time he was adamant: surgery was not indicated and he would not perform it. She was encouraged to accept psychiatric assistance, but refused, and instead found another doctor who felt that she might have some difficulty with stability of her back which could be surgically correctable. She had the surgery and once again was pain free, this time for a period of two months. She again injured her back during strenuous physical activity, and again the pain became worse, severely limiting her physical activity with accompanying depression and irritability.

In the five-year period following her original injury, this woman repeated the above cycle three times. Each time she received temporary relief following unnecessary surgery, and each time she felt the surgery was a small price to pay for relief from pain. At the time she finally consented to psychiatric treatment she was no longer able to convince any doctor of her need for further surgery. Only then was it discerned she had manic-depressive illness. What originally had been a minor back injury kicked off a grim coastering cycle of very real back pain. When the manic-depressive illness was controlled, the pain went away.

HOW TO MANAGE YOUR COASTERING

Along with managing the number of life-change units you accumulate, you should try to view the accomplishment of any task or event as a part of daily living rather than looking at such achievements as "stopping points" or times for "letting down." This is not easy to do in a society that has coined such clichés as "the thrill of victory and the agony of defeat," or "winning isn't everything; it's the only thing." But agonizing over defeats and reveling in victories can be a dangerous life-style.

If your customary manner is type A, fast-paced, try to slow down by mild degrees in a uniform way rather than suddenly embracing total relaxation between outbursts of activity. In the same way, if you are a classic type B, relaxed and calm, try to modestly pick up your life tempo uniformly across periods of both work and play. Ideally, one's coastering pattern would resemble line C on the graph below. However, either coaster A or B are much healthier than coasters X, Y, or Z.

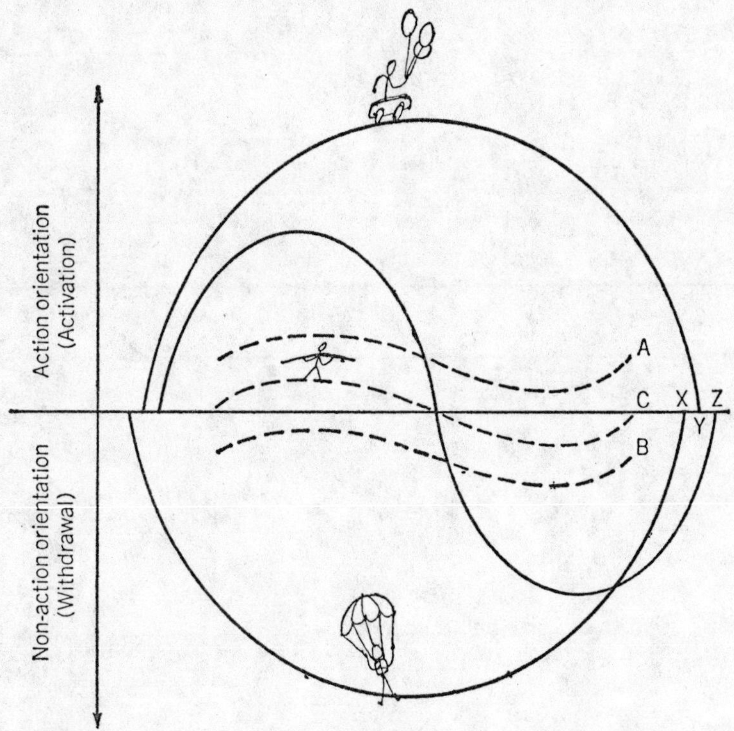

If you perceive you are clearly overactivated, then sensible use of an exercise like the Relaxation Response might very well help. Do not, however, employ a relaxation technique if you are clearly non-action oriented. For instance, *the last thing in the world you need if you are depressed is more non-action orientation.* Instead, get moving. Run around the block, chop wood, go to a baseball game, make love, but don't sit and fret. And drop your meditation class!

If you can achieve the point of view that the goal of life is to be adequate to the tasks ahead, your Colter Coaster will just about manage itself.

CHAPTER 8

THE UPS AND DOWNS OF DISEASE

The number of belief systems we've evolved to aid in the control of disease boggles any reasonable accounting. Dietary fads and restrictions, physical exercises, wearing charms and amulets, religious and quasi-religious ceremonies, warm baths, cold baths, sulfur baths, even mud baths. We inhale vapors, swallow pills, drink teas, apply poultices. We meditate, we perspire, we relax, we jog, we indulge, we abstain. There appears no end to the beliefs and programs we've developed to cope with disease.

In one way or another, most of these systems work.

Some actually make scientific sense but have not yet been studied or recognized by experts. Most work, however, because they help stabilize people's lives. Belief in such practices as maintaining an "organic" diet, doing yoga exercises, or wearing a copper bracelet often provides a central focus around which one can organize life and avoid marked changes in activation. These maneuvers to stabilize may aggravate or even infuriate others, but they represent the only way some of us can cope or continue to function, and they should be recognized as such.

Most of us utilize the professional community to achieve

precisely the same kind of stabilization provided by a belief in vegetarian diets or Hare Krishna. Depending upon our needs and beliefs, we may rely upon a minister, employer, physician, friend, social worker, or teacher. Such people help us maintain stability in our lives through a combination of reassurance, emotional support, medications, problem solving, and sometimes simply "being there" to lean on.

Why is this kind of stability important, whatever the source? Because it influences your ability to avoid and/or survive disease. An unstable life, a life marked by high levels of life change and swings in activation, is not in itself a problem, although it may create unhappiness for you and those around you. But if you have a disease, or any predisposition toward a disease, stabilization may be critical to your survival.

Imagine that your central nervous system (your spine, brain, nerves, and neurochemistry) is a computer programmed to respond in just four ways to changes in your environment: 1) It can increase its activity level; 2) It can decrease its activity level; 3) It can remain unchanged; 4) It can become disorganized. These changes may involve any of your major organ systems–your heart, lungs, skeletal muscles, gastrointestinal system, or your central nervous system itself. Though fanciful, this notion can provide an insight into the link between psychosocial events and psychophysiological changes–the mind-body link. This is the link between life changes, activation and withdrawal, coastering, and disease.

The following disease profiles serve to illustrate some of these complex relationships and their effects.

ANGINA PECTORIS

Some people have a narrowing of the arteries that provide nutrients and oxygen to the heart. When the needs of the heart for oxygen and nutrients are greater than the ability of the impaired arteries to deliver these substances, such patients experience chest pain. To prevent pain, it's necessary to keep the needs of the heart well balanced with the ability of the arteries to deliver oxygen and nutrients and to remove waste material. Among conditions that can be associated with chest pain are euphoria (feeling very good), anger, anxiety, exercise, and emotional tension. These conditions all have in common activation of the skeletal musculature which in turn signals the heart to increase blood supply to the muscles. In these settings, the heart works hard to meet the demands placed on the active skeletal muscles. But it receives no increase in oxygen or nutrients to do the job. The heart runs out of oxygen and nutrients and accumulates waste materials. You then feel pain.

Imagine that this happens to you over a period of several years. Every time you feel euphoric, angry, anxious, or every time you exercise, you suffer chest pain. Feeling good is bad, feeling bad is bad, exercising is bad. You may crawl in a hole and hibernate, while people around you wonder what's wrong with you. Who can possibly understand that feeling too good turns you off? People can't realize you have learned how to avoid activating emotions for a very good reason—they produce chest pain. If you can stabilize your life in a way that allows you to experience these emotions without activating the heart, you will be in much improved shape. This can be accomplished with professional help; however, you can begin to help yourself by noticing what circumstances are associated with chest pain. For instance, there may be naturally occurring situations in which you become activated in the absence of chest pain. If so, learn all you can about them. You may well find that you can use what you have learned as an aid to dealing with the same emotions in other settings.

On the other hand, avoiding all emotions that produce chest pain is not healthy. It is useful to experience a little emotion that is associated with chest pain in order to build your tolerance. The same is true with exercise. Exercising just to the point of chest pain may well increase your ability to exercise. The important thing is to stop the emotion or exercise at the onset of the pain. Then do it again the next day and the next. You may well find you can walk farther and experience more emotion without chest pain after a month or so of exercising.

Unfortunately the issue is not as simple as just avoiding high levels of activation. Many angina patients also have to avoid extreme withdrawal or non-activation—apathy, depression, and at times even extreme drowsiness. Medicine would profit from more information in this realm, but some patients experience chest pain when withdrawn. This may be secondary to decreased blood flow to the heart without a decreased metabolic need of the heart for oxygen and nutrients. As with the activation pattern, exposure to situations producing this pain probably increases the patient's tolerance over time. In many patients the successful treatment of depression alleviates the problem completely.

CONGESTIVE HEART FAILURE

The patient with congestive heart failure shares many problems with angina patients, but also experiences water and sodium accumulation as a result of the heart's not being strong enough to do its job of circulating blood. This often occurs in association with angina pectoris. For this reason, and because of the general weakened condition of the heart, the patient may become worse with either activation or non-activation.

The activating feelings of excitement, uneasiness, apprehension or anger are associated with *excretion* of sodium and water which actually somewhat alleviates congestive heart failure. (The sodium and water accumulation are what cause the congestive patient to experience edema and weight gain.) However, the activation of the heart may cause chest pain or "overwork" a weak heart. But with non-activating feelings such as hopelessness, dejection, exhaustion, and depression there is an *accumulation* of sodium and water and an increase in severity of the congestive heart failure. Therefore, the patient with congestive heart failure may be in an exceedingly tough bind. Any emotion which activates him may either make him worse or better and any emotion which inactivates him makes him worse. As you can imagine, such complicated jockeying of water and sodium takes careful and expert guidance. Again, however, the observant patient will be of great assistance to himself by observing the situations in which he gets worse and better.

MYOCARDIAL INFARCTION[1]

The psychophysiology of myocardial infarct is similar, if not identical, to that of cerebral infarct or stroke described in the previous chapter, but here's a curious thing: many people with severe coronary arteriosclerosis do not develop myocardial infarctions.

The person who is most vulnerable has been under sustained activation for a long period of time and has generally been successful in his or her profession. The activation is interrupted by a real or imagined personal or business failure, or by the conscious decision to slow down.

During activation cardiac output and coronary blood flow are high. In addition, the viscosity of the blood tends to be high and clotting time relatively low. When the activation suddenly stops, the viscosity of the blood, clotting time, cardiac output, and coronary blood flow all change. However, *changes in the viscosity of the blood and clotting time do not occur as fast as changes in cardiac output and coronary blood flow*. There is a lag during which a period of maximum vulnerability occurs: coronary blood flow is lowered in a setting of elevated blood viscosity and lowered clotting time. This is when an infarction is postulated to develop.

The typical infarction occurs in our most productive people. A classic example is provided by a professor and chairman of medicine at a major university.

This physician had been productive and hard-working all of his adult life. He had published a host of scientific papers, a

[1] A myocardial infarction occurs when a blood clot restricts blood flow through a coronary artery, thus killing a portion of the heart muscle.

dozen textbooks, and he was an international leader in his field. Between the ages of twenty-five and fifty he rarely worked less than eighty hours each week, and he delighted in outdistancing his colleagues. Despite his workload he maintained an active social life. He never seemed to tire. He was a popular, contented, productive person.

The year he turned fifty he attempted to rise from departmental chairman to dean of another medical school. The medical school was one of the most prestigious in the country, and candidates for the position of dean were all departmental chairmen with backgrounds roughly equivalent to his. Our chairman was not chosen for the post; instead someone of equal stature who had an Ivy League background was selected. Our chairman became angry, resentful, and withdrawn.

He began to spend less time working, and sometimes he didn't show up for work at all. Attempts on the part of colleagues to communicate these concerns with him were met with rigid denials that there was any problem. He literally seemed to go into professional hibernation. He seemed to interpret his failure to advance as a sign that he had lost the ability to compete.

In truth, it was the first and only major administrative or political setback he had ever experienced. After one month of withdrawal he developed an acute myocardial infarction and died.

HYPERVENTILATION AND HYPOVENTILATION SYNDROMES

Hyperventilation syndrome is probably the most common diagnosis attributed to people who are anxious, fearful, angry, or experiencing a combination of these action-oriented emotions. Ordinarily, when we become activated we breathe more air as our muscles tense in preparation for action. In the absence of lung disease, the increase in air movement occurs faster than increases in muscle tension. When this happens there is a fall in the concentration of carbon dioxide in arterial blood. In most people the carbon dioxide tension does not fall to levels that produce symptoms.

People with hyperventilation syndrome appear to lose control of the emotional activation to the point where increases in metabolism (increased muscle tension which produces carbon dioxide) are not sufficient to keep the arterial carbon dioxide tension from dropping into the symptom-producing range. The result is "air hunger." As the carbon dioxide tension falls, the patient becomes short of breath, lightheaded, and may experience strange feelings over the skin, dizziness, chest pain, chills, and sweating. These symptoms of course frighten the patient, and thereby even further increase activation and the symptoms.

A common mistake is to confuse the hyperventilation syndrome with what can be described as the hypoventilation syndrome. It is not uncommon to find someone who will complain of shortness of breath with depression. Shortness of breath has been so firmly associated with hyperventilation by physicians that the possibility of hypoventilation with shortness of breath has been largely ignored. The differentiation is important since the way to treat hyperventilation syndrome is to decrease the action orientation by medications or psychotherapy. However, if these same treatment techniques are utilized with patients with the hypoventilation syndrome, they will get worse. They need to be activated with medications or other techniques. This is because the shortness of breath they experience is associated with a decrease in the movement of air. The person with hypoventilation syndrome is underbreathing and the person with hyperventilation syndrome is overbreathing.

ESSENTIAL HYPERTENSION

Essential hypertension (high blood pressure with no "organically" explainable cause) occurs in association with an increase in the constriction of peripheral arteries along with an accompanying resistance to blood flow. Most patients with high blood pressure of this type have a "hypertensive attitude." They feel something is threatening them; they have to be ready for anything. This is an attitude that has been likened to the response of the vascular system to threatened blood loss during "flight or fight" stress reactions. Some researchers feel certain that the sustained increase in peripheral resistance is symbolic of a sustained threat of blood loss with a protective shunting of blood to vital internal organs. In essence, this is an adaptive mechanism gone astray. It is only useful when there is an actual threat of having your body cut or torn.

People who are particularly vulnerable to high blood pressure are those who feel threatened by the environment and cannot talk effectively about it or change the environment. One group of patients typifying this are those who are continually suspicious or paranoid. An extreme example is provided by the case history of a twenty-eight-year-old man with paranoid schizophrenia. This patient developed hypertension at the age of twenty, and by the time he was twenty-two his blood-pressure averages were 240/120.[2] At age twenty-five his readings were averaging 250/130, and at age twenty-eight his readings varied from 240/130 to 250/150. These levels are dangerous, but despite intensive treatment of his hypertension, the blood-pressure readings remained high. Finally the paranoia was controlled and the pressure readings dropped to a more acceptable level or about 240/120 (which is still high).

Relaxation exercises appear helpful in lowering blood pressure, though only modestly so. Still, any reduction in elevated blood pressure is desirable. And there is evidence that relaxation exercises may diminish feelings of being threatened.

[2] Normal blood pressure is relative to age, time of day, physical activity, and other components. As a generalization, a systolic reading of 100 to 160 is normal range; a diastolic reading of 60 to 100. Thus a young man of twenty-two might normally have a reading of, say, 140/80.

MUSCLE TENSION HEADACHE

This pain occurs in much the same manner as back pain, described in Chapter 7. It is the fixation of the head for action that is the key. The pain occurs in a setting of emotional and skeletal muscle activation. We obviously couldn't have our heads flopping around when we engaged in strenuous physical activity. As with back pain, the muscles tense, waste products accumulate, and pain results. Treatment aimed at relaxation can be effective, since the more relaxed you are, the less chance there is for pain to occur.

A serious problem emerges when a migraine headache is diagnosed as a tension headache. As we've explained, a migraine patient who is encouraged to relax at the wrong time will have more frequent and severe headaches. It is terribly important not to confuse these two different kinds of head pain. Relaxation for the migraine-prone individual can be, at best, a painful idea.

VASOVAGAL FAINTING

The fainting occurs in a setting in which there is a sustained increase in activation with an increasing pulse rate, blood pressure, and peripheral resistance. But unlike the patient with hypertension, this patient's peripheral resistance increase is not permanent. With the sudden ending of activation (when a needle is pulled out of a vein, for example, or an intimidating medical procedure is terminated) the tone of the sympathetic nervous system drops markedly, but the opposing vagal tone is normal or increased.[3] There is a sudden loss of blood flow (the heart actually stops pumping for a few seconds), the blood supply to that part of the brain that keeps you awake is shut off, and you faint.

In some patients the heart may stop for fifteen to twenty

[3] Vasovagal fainting is a common occurrence among donors to blood banks.

seconds. Attempts to revive the person with a vasovagal faint by standing him on his feet before sympathetic tone returns to normal will invariably lead to another faint.

This is another example of an acute phenomenon associated with sudden relief or relaxation following an activating event, much like migraine headache.

EMPHYSEMA

With this disease the patient is vexed by both activation and non-activation. Many activating emotions require that an emphysema patient's lungs pump more air than the lungs are able to because of the disease. Since the muscular system is usually not impaired, the more activated the patient becomes, the more oxygen he needs and the less able he is to deliver it. A second problem is related to a lag between the onset of ventilation changes and the onset of changes in skeletal-muscle activity. With depression or other non-activating emotions there is a drop in the amount of air the patient breathes. However, there is no such rapid drop in the need to supply oxygen and nutrients to the muscles. Because of this, the patient is once again delivering less air than is required to take care of the body's needs.

Patients with severe emphysema may have a deficit in ventilation that is so severe they can barely keep going even when resting quietly. Any change in metabolic demand will lead to the rapid onset of symptoms (severe shortness of breath). As a result, like patients with severe cardiac disease, they may avoid any emotionally charged or personally related life experiences.

It's hardly surprising that the patient with emphysema may be difficult to handle emotionally. He or she may experience severe shortness of breath with joy, loving feelings, anger, anxiety, depression, or sadness. Any and all emotions or feelings may be associated with unpleasant symptoms. This isn't easy for a family who come to assume that a spouse or parent no longer loves them because loving feelings are no longer expressed. But understanding the problem, from both sides of it, can help.

ASTHMA

Asthma is similar to emphysema in some ways; however, there is an important difference. In most asthmatics the inability to move air is temporary and can be alleviated by bronchodilators, steroids, or other techniques. When the patient is in the midst of a severe asthma attack, his reactions are essentially those of the patient with severe emphysema.

The type of behavioral pattern that fits many asthmatics is similar to that shown by manic-depressive patients. The asthma attack occurs in a setting of increasing activation or shortly after the activation has stopped. The activation occurs in a setting of helplessness and feeling "shut out." As these feeling states increase in intensity, there is an increase in mucus production in the bronchi, mucosal swelling, and finally smooth-muscle contraction. The attack is followed by a period of withdrawal. During this period of withdrawal the patient tends to develop an infection somewhere in the respiratory system. The infection occurs at the period in the disease when the patient is becoming increasingly activated and infection is thereby usually implicated in producing the new attack. This implication may or may not be so, since the swings in mood seem to occur with or without an infection.

Many asthmatics are pleasantly surprised when stopping swings in activation terminates their difficulty with asthma or renders their asthma completely controllable.

SCHIZOPHRENIA

Imagine yourself in a situation where all the environmental inputs increased by as much as five times, and that this assault on your central nervous system continued for months or even years. Information would be coming in at a rate that you couldn't possibly assimilate and yet the barrage would continue, night and day, week after week after week. What would you do?

When environmental inputs become too great in the normal person, he or she is subject to a condition called "input flooding," an experience common to residents of large cities. Such individuals deal with incoming data in less and less detail until finally they will respond only to specific meaningful inputs or instructions. In an environment of input-flooded people, even a cry for help may be ignored unless it is specifically aimed. When you are attacked in such a setting it is seldom enough to merely scream for assistance. Instead, you must say, "You in the blue jacket, help me!" If this recommendation sounds haunting, it came to light as the result of a 1964 study which examined the reasons why Catherine Genovese did not receive help while being murdered by a maniac who took over a half hour to inflict multiple knife wounds as she screamed and struggled on a New York City street. No one among thirty-eight onlookers came to her aid or called the police. She probably could have saved her life by pointing to someone and specifically asking for help. Keep in mind, these were "normal" people who watched the woman die.

In the schizophrenic we deal with someone who continuously or intermittently receives so much afferent input that he appears to continuously experience input flooding. Thus it's possible to explain many of the problems experienced by the schizophrenic as originating with increased afferent input. This helps offer insights into schizophrenic withdrawal, agitation, hallucinations, and delusions. There are only a limited number of ways one can respond to increased afferent stimuli. The withdrawal may represent an attempt to isolate oneself from the environment, thus reducing the input. The wild activation may be a direct response to the input. The hallucinations and delusions may be attempts to fill gaps in information as input is dealt with in less and less detail. To be sure, this is a fanciful way to look at schizophrenia, but it is useful;

what's more, it is consistent with how acute schizophrenia is clinically treated at the present time.

The acute paranoid schizophrenic scans the environment intensively and extensively, and although "wide open" to extraneous stimuli, he cannot focus his attention. He is constantly being overloaded by sensory information.

The non-paranoid schizophrenic does not specifically scan the environment. The sensory defect appears to stem from hypersensitivity to ordinary stimuli with a complete "shutting out" of strong sensory stimuli.

In either case, the problem could well be the result of increases in sensitivity or disorganization in specific parts of the brain rather than an increase in actual transmission of information. Regardless, the new medications for treatment of schizophrenia seem to decrease sensory input and terminate the acute attack information.

MANIC-DEPRESSIVE PSYCHOSIS

In 1949, an Australian physician named John Cade made medical history with some seemingly ridiculous experiments and no budget. The upshot was the introduction of lithium salts into clinical psychiatry. But it took another twenty years before it was finally conceded by most clinical researchers that lithium carbonate was a specific treatment for manic-depressive illness, because the original data were so suspicious.

Traditionally, manic-depressive illness has described patients with cyclic episodes of depression and mania. More recently the term has been applied to both recurrent depressive episodes and recurrent manic episodes without swings in the opposite directions. These are called unipolar depression or unipolar mania when either condition is recurrent. The classic cyclic illness is called bipolar.

It is now established that the bipolar and some of the unipolar conditions are completely reversible with maintenance lithium carbonate. The lithium does not appear to have any significant side effects at therapeutic levels. Its main effect is simply that of stopping the wide swings in activity. It flattens the "coaster," and it restores patients to comfort and productivity.

Wide swings from physical and mental inactivity to physical and mental hyperactivity are associated with a vast array of physiological changes. Problems confronting a researcher who is attempting to find basic physiologic changes which may be responsible for the illness are thereby greatly complicated by the need to work out the "normal psychophysiology" of the illness first. An identical problem occurs in examining schizophrenia, but it is not as apparent. In both cases, the burden of explanation frequently relies on *neurotransmitters,* a complex group of biochemical substances (neurochemical precursors, active transmitters, enzymes, etc.) that transmit information to, through, and from the central nervous system.

One explanation, for instance, is the "Catecholamine Hypothesis," a theory about mania and depression supported by the analysis of changes in catecholamines secreted in patients' urine samples during episodes of depression and mania. Excretion of these transmitters increases during episodes of mania and decreases during periods of depression. When treated for depression with anti-depressant medication, the excretion of transmitters increases; the excretion decreases during treatments for mania. From this evidence the Catecholamine Hypothesis concludes that it is the quantity of transmitters that causes the disease.

This is akin to measuring a diabetic's blood sugar and concluding that glucose causes diabetes!

It's likely that increases and decreases in neurotransmitters associated with manic-depressive psychosis are reflections of other changes in the central nervous system and are produced by the disease process. In any event, they certainly are not the cause of the disease. Psychiatric diseases produce many physiologic and biochemical abnormalities which are side effects of the diseases. Unfortunately they do not always give us clues to the mechanisms which cause the disorders, but we're certain they are *not the cause* of psychiatric illnesses.

What the data on neurotransmitters seem to indicate is that there is indeed some defect or alteration of nerve transmission with the development of depression and mania. The defect is reversible with currently available treatment. However, the disease mechanism remains uncertain.

DEPRESSION

Few diseases are as commonly misunderstood as depression. To many, the grief experienced after death of a loved one, or the sadness experienced with breakup of a marriage, or the feeling of listlessness experienced when emotionally overloaded . . . these represent depression. Indeed, for short periods of time they may seem like depression. However to a psychiatrist, depression is the term increasingly applied to a specific kind of disease.

Depression is characterized by absolute *hopelessness*. The person with depression feels that nothing can be done to help. It is not just "there is nothing I can do," which characterizes helplessness, a condition patients may pass through when getting depressed. Helplessness implies that although there is nothing that the patient can do, there is something that someone else can do to correct things. With hopelessness, the patient feels there is nothing he or she can do and nothing anyone else can do either. The despair is unbending.

The signs and symptoms that characterize patients with a significant clinical depression fall into two categories: "retarded" and "agitated." The person with a retarded depression may feel like sleeping continuously, have no energy, be unable to interact with life, be unable to concentrate, feel suicidal, and be constipated. The person with an agitated depression may experience insomnia, constipation, suicidal drive, low spirits, irritability, inability to concentrate, and nervousness.

Many ways are currently popular for classifying depression;

the *agitated* and *retarded* categories are useful for illustration because they are the most common clinical presentation of depression. Fortunately, both categories respond to appropriate antidepressant medications.

Another consideration is that depression can be "masked," that is, it may present itself as pain, symptoms in an organ system other than central-nervous, or as changes in behavior. Agitated depression is felt by some researchers to be secondary to the brain attempting to compensate for the loss of activation that characterizes a retarded depression. In other words, people who are able to compensate develop an agitated depression. The agitation compensates for the loss of energy, but it's not useful activation, and the person with such a depression state remains incapacitated. Patients with this kind of depression have an added disadvantage in that they have the energy to commit suicide. Patients with retarded depression may want to kill themselves but lack the energy.

TUBERCULOSIS

This is a disease which has a specific etiologic factor—the bacteria *Mycobacterium tuberculosis*. What could be simpler? The patient is exposed to the bacteria and thereby develops the disease. However, as with most infectious diseases, tuberculosis is enormously responsive to psychosocial variables—life changes and coping abilities. This was recognized even before the discovery of antibiotic therapy. In 1905, Joseph Hersey Pratt, a Boston internist, developed the first organized group educational and psychotherapeutic method of treatment in this country. He developed it for treatment of tuberculosis patients and soon found that patients treated by this method got well faster than those who did not receive the treatment. Today we call what Dr. Pratt developed *group psychotherapy*, and it is popularly recognized as the property of the psychiatrist. Yet, it wasn't until about 1921, when as a direct result of Pratt's work, St. Elizabeths Hospital in Washington, D.C., instituted group therapy for treatment of chronic schizophrenic patients. Curiously, only from that point on did group therapy continue to develop in psychiatry and disappear from use in the specialty of internal medicine.

Tuberculosis in many ways illustrates the classic infectious disease. It develops in people who have difficulty in adjusting to a prevailing culture and, in the process, are continually overwhelmed and helpless to act. Although this kind of non-activating response to the current scene may increase your probability for contracting any infectious disease, in the natural history of tuberculosis, there are genetic factors as well. In general, the portion of our population born between 1880 and 1920 are those who have reported most tuberculosis disease for the past seventy years. People born after 1920 have a high degree of immunity to tuberculosis. The high tuberculosis rate in people over sixty indicates that tuberculosis is still of epidemic proportion in the older age groups. *This has not changed with the onset of antibiotic therapy for tuberculosis.*

It is of considerable epidemiologic importance that mortality from tuberculosis began to decline prior to the introduction of antibiotics. It is assumed that the disease is running its course in our population. When the last of the people highly susceptible to the disease have died it will become a disease of low incidence unless another population is born of similar susceptibility.

Antibiotics aid in the control of infectious diseases, but there is some question as to whether or not they change the natural history of infectious diseases in our culture. The natural history of most infectious diseases may depend more on our developing natural resistance to the diseases than on the introduction of new antibiotics to "control" each disease.

LUNG CANCER

After the heroic research of recent years, it's difficult to embrace a psychosocial component to lung cancer, yet it appears that psychosocial influences have much to do with this disease. Findings published in 1963, by Dr. David Kissen, strongly suggest that lung-cancer patients have some characteristic psychosocial profiles. They have a lower than average incidence of childhood emotional disorders coupled with a high rate of concealment or bottling up of emotional difficulties. In other words, they can engage neither in activation nor non-activation. The end result appears to be a cancer. In Dr. Kissen's words: ". . . Lung cancer patients have a poor outlet for emotional discharge and tend to conceal or bottle up their emotional difficulties."

This factor has been apparent enough for Dr. Kissen to accurately identify lung-cancer patients with a clinical interview in the absence of any previous knowledge about their chest lesions.

BLOOD CANCER

Studies reported by Dr. William Green at the Rochester Medical School point to a connection between leukemia in children and psychosocial variables. He found that children with leukemia often had experienced the loss of a loved one by death. One could speculate that the ensuing feelings of hopelessness and loss in the child reduce the immunologic tolerance of the body and allow the development of abnormal numbers of blood cells. Whatever the reason, the association exists. Dr. Stanley E. Fischman, a California psychiatrist who specializes in working with seriously ill children, says, "Frequently, when we explore the recent background of a child with leukemia we learn the youngster has suffered some kind of extreme loss, the death of a parent or sibling, or a major social setback, such as being unexpectedly held back in school."

"Chance might account for this," adds Dr. Fischman, "but I doubt it."

BREAST CANCER

Work by Dr. James Henry at the University of Southern California indicates that cancer of the breast in certain types of mice develops after a breakdown of the social system in the cage in which the animals are kept. It was the impression of the experimenters that the mice which developed carcinoma were "depressed." If so, they might well have some reduction in immunology defenses to the development of carcinoma. At the present time there is no way of making definitive statements in this area; however, accumulating research indicates that the development of cancer may not be quite the unpredictable and unfathomable event it is traditionally felt to be.

ULCERATIVE COLITIS

This disease is characterized by inflammation of the lower intestine; the wall of the colon. Once established, the disease is greatly aggravated by activating feeling states such as anger and resentment. These feelings produce hyperfunction of the colon manifested by increased motility, increased blood flow, and the secretion of enzymes which destroy the lining of the colon. With sustained feelings of anger and resentment, and the associated hyperfunction of the colon, there results bleeding and ulceration of the colon which leads to bloody diarrhea and abdominal pain.

Colitis patients often learn early in the disease to avoid activating emotions. Any procedure which places them in a position of experiencing activating emotions produces increased problems and they will go to great extremes to avoid such activation. A common mistake with such patients (and other chronic disease patients) is to use a therapeutic technique which uncovers their emotional problems and thereby leads to activation and increasing disease. In order to employ psychotherapy with such patients, it is important not to activate them in ways that increase their symptoms. Otherwise, they will begin to refuse medical assistance, and justifiably so.

DIABETES MELLITUS

The first observed relationship between diabetes mellitus and changes in activation extends back to Sir Thomas Willis, in 1674. He noted that patients with diabetes had sweeter urine when they were depressed. The relationship between depression and diabetes has been the subject of much speculation since that time. Studies by Dr. Peter Mueller of Rutgers have shown that there are significant changes in the utilization of glucose and insulin during depression. Some patients have clinical diabetes only when depressed and inactivated. When they are hyperactive the abnormality of glucose metabolism disappears.

A dramatic example of the relationship between changes in activation and diabetes is supplied by the history of the wife of a business executive. Her insulin need varied from over 100 units to 0 units per day. Understandably, she was considered to be a "brittle" diabetic. She also had manic-depressive illness. During periods of depression she needed over 100 units of insulin for control. During the periods of mania her insulin need was 0. This was a terrible problem since the swings from mania to depression or depression to mania tended to be rather sudden. When the swings were from depression to mania, she required hospitalization for insulin shock (hypoglycemia induced by insulin overdose). When the swings were from mania to depression, she required hospitalization for diabetic ketoacidosis (not enough insulin). As a result of treatment of the manic-depressive illness with lithium carbonate, her insulin need settled down to about 20 units per day, and she no longer had difficulty with insulin shock or diabetic ketoacidosis. This is an uncommonly dramatic diabetes case history, but also a classic illustration of the kinds of medical miseries that may develop when a combination of uncontrolled variations in physiological stability occur in combination with a recognized disease entity.

WHAT ARE WE TRYING TO SAY?

The diseases sketched here hardly represent a current survey of medicine; however, they serve to illustrate a point of view about illness that can be invaluable to you.

Observe the relationships between your physiological reactions to life events and to your emotional ups and downs. *You are your own best scientific laboratory.* Your observations about yourself can provide important information to help you avoid disease or to help in the treatment of disease. Such observations can provide you with the means to make your life more comfortable and more productive.

CHAPTER 9

THE ART OF BEING SUCCESSFULLY SICK

All of us, laymen and physicians alike, tend to confuse the symptoms of illness with illness itself, but they are not the same.

You may have a disease, or several diseases, and not be sick. Differently, you may be terribly sick and have no disease. The explanation for this paradox is that culturally we interpret being sick as experiencing a loss of comfort and/or productivity. You may have essential hypertension, a disease, with no loss of comfort or productivity. During a heat wave you may feel terribly sick, uncomfortable and unproductive, with no disease present. Your neighbor, the schizophrenic, may well be the most comfortable fellow in town, but also wholly unproductive.

Understanding that sickness and disease are not the same thing is paramount to successfully living with illness, especially chronic and recurring illness, because *you are almost certainly not as sick as you think you are.*

SYMPTOMS AND SIGNS

When you consult your doctor, he looks for *signs* and *symptoms* of illness. Symptoms are subjective feelings, the discomforts that worried you enough to visit your doctor in the first place. Common symptoms are pain, dyspnea (shortness of breath), fatigue, itching, delusions, hallucinations, and depression. Signs of illness are mainly objective; broken bones, cuts, abnormal laboratory tests, strange behavior. The signs of illness frequently accompany symptoms, but not always.

With the disease schizophrenia, signs of illness may be strange behavior or changes in brain neurochemistry; the symptoms may appear as believing things that are not true (delusions), or seeing, hearing, or feeling things that are not here (hallucinations). Most of us are conditioned to avoid anyone with these symptoms. They frighten us because they don't fit our popular idea of what illness should be. They appear dangerous. In fact, the danger may or may not be real. A group of schizophrenic patients is no more dangerous than any random sample of people from the general population.

We also have a difficult time believing schizophrenics are "really sick." They sometimes present themselves as very comfortable but absolutely unproductive. Such people are commonly regarded as malingerers and are often treated with hostility.

Advances in laboratory diagnosis of diseases produce other sorts of problems. It is easy to understand you are ill if you have severe leg pain and your leg is bent at an unusual angle. It's obviously broken. But what if you feel well, comfortable, and productive, yet have an electrocardiogram that indicates heart disease, a chest X ray showing carcinoma, a blood test disclosing diabetes mellitus, or a pap smear that points to cancer of the cervix? Subsequently you're told a devastating disease is present for which you must take the word of your doctor and submit to treatment you don't understand. In these circumstances "well" patients are subjected to radical medical and surgical procedures. Few of us adjust easily to this. We need to "feel sick" if something is physically wrong, and in this kind of setting many people begin acting sick simply to communicate the severity of their illnesses. Developing a carcinoma is a life-threatening situation, but others will not understand this unless you act sick in addition to having the physical signs of disease. Without this cultural expression of illness, the carcinoma patient must face a potentially devastating situation alone. Few of us choose to do that.

Another clinical situation can be equally distressing. You may find yourself with a symptom of disease but no sign of disease, for example severe lower back pain with no "medical" explanation for it. Examination after examination is performed without positive findings. There is simply "no reason" for your pain. What can you do? Should you grin and bear it while awaiting a medical breakthrough that will demonstrate a heretofore unknown physical abnormality? Should that happen, you can be appropriately ill. If it doesn't happen, however, you may find yourself in a situation where people will not believe that you experience pain, or they will suggest the pain is "all in your head." In this situation it's helpful to remember all pain is in your head. Without a head you couldn't feel pain, or anything else for that matter.

Unfortunately, pain without a sign may lead to alienation from your doctor and increasing reliance on less traditional or even phony treatment. When this occurs it is essential to be associated with an understanding and tolerant physician who will allow you to try different and even unorthodox treatments but who will also stand by you and care for any serious trouble resulting from the pain or treatments.

To be sure, modern medicine does not have all the answers. But neither does any other profession or group of healers. Situations in which incurable symptoms or disease are encountered should be met maturely, and the limitations of treatment spelled out. You and your physician can then be comfortable with each other and arrange the best possible management of the symptoms and signs.

The following review of common symptoms that alert us to diseases can be useful in understanding the nature of sickness. Most of these symptoms are non-specific; experiencing them does not tell you exactly what the illness is. They simply alert you to the need for taking some action. Depending on your background and inclination, you may consult a friend, a physician, a minister, or someone else. By tradition these symptoms send us to a doctor in our culture; however, that is not true among subsections of our culture, and it isn't true in many other cultures of the world.

PAIN

Pain is the symptom we all associate with being sick or needing medical attention. In general, the more severe pain is interpreted, the more serious patients and doctors consider the disease. Pain is almost always analyzed as uncomfortable and dangerous. Still, no matter how articulate the patient and/or sophisticated the doctor, *the only test of pain's severity is the patient's report*. Unlike most other sensations (hearing, smell, sight), pain cannot be shared by the examiner. The amount of pain experienced is strictly evaluated by the patient, and there is usually no way for a doctor to confirm the presence or absence of pain.

Avoidance of pain has played a profound role in our evolution. Since prehistoric times, we have searched for ways to deal with pain and pain-producing situations. So instilled in us is pain as a danger signal that its presence in even small and innocent amounts triggers massive physiological reactions throughout our nervous systems.

In some situations pain is only felt after we learn an event is dangerous. A sad and frequent example is the patient with terminal cancer who feels no pain until the diagnosis is made. For the rest of this patient's life pain may be his constant companion. In this situation pain symbolizes the nature of danger and reminds those around the patient that his condition is critical. Too often pain is the *only* avenue of communication open to terminal patients. It's usually not possible for a terminal patient to discuss his fear of dying with others; such candor drives people away (doctors, nurses, family, friends, even clergy) and leaves the patient to cope by himself. Everyone is willing to talk about pain, however, and it can therefore symbolize others' fear of dying. Thus the patient can be treated and sympathized with for his pain rather than his real feelings. The pain provides a focus, a symbol more comfortable than the reality of dying.

In contrast to a common notion that the more pain there is the worse the injury or disease, much evidence indicates that the intensity of pain is mostly dependent on the social situation in which it is incurred. Men wounded seriously in combat often experience little or no pain. Persons suffering similar injuries in a car accident, in which their car is struck by someone obviously drunk, will feel severe pain. In this case the sense of being hurt is intensified by the injustice of the situation. Car-accident victims are hurt emotionally as well as physically,[1] and the subsequent pain, given the same injuries, is considerably greater than for battlefield wounds.

Pain is a serious management problem when it becomes chronic, regardless of the initiating cause. Pain may produce a complicated mix of detrimental emotional and physical changes. These frequently emerge as depression, anger, cardiac changes, respiratory changes, gastrointestinal changes, and kidney changes. Pain may actually associate with and/or produce tissue damage.

Despite the elusive nature of pain, much is known about the way pain is transmitted from the skin or internal organs to the brain. Anatomic and physiologic studies can accurately trace nerve pathways that give us the ability to feel pain. But, alas, knowing the pathways does not help you or your physician in a clinical situation. Pain remains a subjective sensation.

For the same individual, pain from a specific region of the body may be perceived as excruciating on one occasion and nonexistent on another, even though the painful stimulus is

[1] Given the current state of our medical language, it is difficult to avoid this kind of linguistic parallelism.

identical on both occasions. Identical pain stimuli will be perceived in vastly different ways by two people from dissimilar cultural backgrounds. Scientific evidence highlights the fact that these differences are not a result of differing nerve pathways, but rather a result of the astonishing control higher centers of your brain exercise over your ability to feel pain.

If you experience consistent pain, or a painful condition that is intermittent, it may be helpful and constructive to keep track of your pain's intensity and its relationship to the way you feel during the occurrence of life events. The three scales that conclude this chapter can help you to do this. It is also useful to remember that pain is something *you feel*. It is there, if you feel it, but no one else can feel it or define it for you. As you'll discover, however, *almost always when you compare your present level of pain with the most pain you've ever experienced, you are more comfortable than you think you are.*

DYSPNEA

Dyspnea is a common symptom in patients with and without pulmonary disease. Its identification is based on the subjective judgment of the patient and is generally not definable in terms of blood gases or ventilatory abnormalities. Patients vary in their descriptions of dyspnea, but the general complaint is that of uncomfortable sensations arising in the chest or airways which are interpreted as interference with normal breathing. The patient feels smothered, breathless, and that not enough air is available. Some patients experience severe dyspnea with little or no structural change in their cardiopulmonary systems, while other patients experience mild dyspnea, or no dyspnea at all, with severe structural change. Dyspnea is sometimes experienced by normal, healthy people during strenuous exercise and periods of emotion.

When people prone to dyspnea attacks are studied in detail, it is found that dyspnea is associated with both emotions that connote activation and emotions that connote non-activation.

With non-activating emotions such as depression, dyspnea is associated with decreased ventilation or hypoventilation. With action-oriented emotions such as anger or anxiety, dyspnea occurs in association with hyperpnea or hyperventilation (increased ventilation). Thus, dyspnea is associated with both increased and decreased ventilation.

As an illness symptom, dyspnea remains confusing. Both healthy people and cardiopulmonary patients experience it. But not all cardiopulmonary patients experience it, and either a relative increase or decrease in ventilation may trigger it. The best explanation for this is that dyspnea is a learned symptom; it depends upon past conditioning experiences. Events such as breath holding or excessive crying during childhood, congestive heart failure, allergic reactions, and bronchial infections apparently lead to physiologic reactions that are perceived as threatening experiences in which dyspnea occurs. In other words, people who suffer dyspnea attacks are hypersensitive to changes in their cardiopulmonary systems. They experience a sort of psychobiologic drowning, a respiratory short circuit. Other people are unaware of these changes and do not suffer the dyspnea symptoms. And, as with so many other illness symptoms, emotional reactions to dyspnea attacks often trigger more and worse dyspnea attacks.

Here then is some startling but helpful information. *The common symptom dyspnea is independent of disease, it is self-perpetuating, and it is a conditioned response.*

Since dyspnea is associated with danger in only two organ systems, it is not widely recognized as so general a danger symptom as pain. Hence if you experience dyspnea, you may be called a malingerer. People around you will often not understand the reason for your inability to work or play; therefore, you may have difficult social relations unless your dyspnea becomes severe enough to be interpreted by others as being painful. Nevertheless, there are three important differences between dyspnea and pain: 1) Dyspnea is not a generalized danger sign; 2) There are no specific nerve pathways that have been demonstrated to reliably produce dyspnea, i.e., dyspnea must be learned or there must be cardiac or pulmonary disease present to initiate it; and 3) Dyspnea is closely associated with physical activity.

If you experience dyspnea, you should remain physically active unless your physician has identified a problem that prohibits it. As patients with dyspnea exercise, they learn that the dyspnea is tolerable and is not a life threat.

The more you exercise, the more control you will have over the dyspnea, and the less threatening the symptom will be.

ITCHING

Itching is a sensation limited to the skin. It's usually defined as the urge to scratch, and it indicates damage to the outer layer of the skin. It's a symptom that tells you something specific about the region in which a problem exists, as well as something about the problem itself. Itching is different from being ticklish, which represents a response to stimulating the skin.

Itching seems to be carried in some of the same nerve fibers that transmit pain, and indeed severe itching may be painful to the extreme. It may be caused by a number of diseases which effect the skin directly or indirectly. For example, you may itch because your skin has been exposed to a toxic chemical such as lye or poison-oak resin. Or you may itch because your skin is exposed to a high level of waste products in the blood, the result of failing kidneys. There are many diseases associated with itching, and the cause should be diagnosed by an appropriately trained physician.

A lot of self-diagnosis and home remedies stem from itching symptoms, most of them faulty, and some of them absolutely bizarre.

FATIGUE

Fatigue is another non-specific symptom that leads us to seek professional help. Often it points to depression, a sort of having had enough of life's problems for a while. This is literally why many college freshmen cannot get out of bed for their early morning classes. Weariness can also indicate other illnesses. Fatigue often occurs when your body is infected, or has reduced levels of the "activation" hormones. Fatigue can accompany any impairment in the biochemical delivery of nourishment or oxygen to the body, or the removal of waste material. And fatigue may indicate the growth of a tumor.

In other words, fatigue can be a symptom of a dysfunction of almost any organ or organ system in your body, and as a symptom it requires expert attention.

HALLUCINATIONS

During certain kinds of medical problems the central nervous system invents sensations for us to experience–sights, sounds, feelings, or odors that are not really there. This seems to occur when we are not paying much attention to our surroundings or are experiencing some disease which shuts off sensation to the brain. Without sensations telling what is real and what is not, the brain fills with things that we think might or should be there.

Combinations of danger, loneliness, and fatigue may trigger hallucinations, circumstances exemplified by Robert Manry's solo voyage across the Atlantic on a thirteen-foot sailboat in 1965. In his book *Tinkerbelle,* describing the adventure, Manry detailed recurring and bizarre hallucinations during his thirty-four-day ocean crossing.

DELUSIONS

Delusions are thoughts that are not true. For example, with some diseases people may think they are exceedingly wealthy or that someone is trying to kill them. These illnesses are usually psychiatric in nature, and they should be evaluated and treated by psychiatrists.

Both delusions and hallucinations are associated with schizophrenia, manic-depressive illness, depression, or diseases of old age, such as organic brain disease. Also, any condition that significantly alters the physical structure or balance of electrolytes or hormones in the brain may produce these symptoms, and they need to be ruled out by a trained physician before any psychiatric treatment program is begun.

FEEDBACK

Here is a helpful way of looking at the complex interplay of psychobiologic factors that perpetuate the symptoms and signs of illness:

I PRIMARY INPUT

Life changes or internal changes (bacterial invasion, divorce, change in culture, hormonal imbalance, etc.)

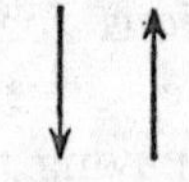

II SECONDARY INPUT

Initial psychologic, biologic, and symptomatic response (pain, dyspnea, confusion, anger, tissue swelling, blood loss, etc.)

III TERTIARY INPUT

Secondary reaction (muscle spasm, hyperventilation, anger, depression, etc.)

Once inputs II and III are in operation, the primary input can be removed (treated, resolved, ended) and the symptoms and signs may continue. When this happens, inputs II and III must be evaluated and dealt with in order to get well.

If inputs II and III (or III and IV, etc.) cannot be managed, the result will be chronic illness.

CHRONIC ILLNESS

We live in a self-styled cut-and-dried sort of culture, a social-political environment businessmen describe as pragmatic, political leaders think of as practical, scientists like to quantify, and some religious teachers interpret as fundamental. In various ways these points of view have insinuated themselves into our attitudes about health. In this cut-and-dried environment, "you acquire a disease, the disease is treated, then the disease goes away." Yet most diseases do not go away. Most of us, sooner or later, develop chronic diseases and have to live with them for the rest of our lives. Nevertheless, our society is geared to deal with acute disease, not to maintain people with chronic disease. There are few courses taught in medical schools aimed at dealing with chronic disease, even though chronic illness is our number one health problem.

Why isn't chronic disease fashionable? The answer lies, in part, with our inability to accept relationships that are not mutally rewarding on a relatively quick basis. Patients with acute heart attacks are treated, rapidly rehabilitated, and returned to productive life. Both patients and doctors are pleased with each other. However, if a heart-attack patient develops chronic and unremitting chest pain, there is no immediate reward for treating him. The symptoms do not go away. There is no admiring patient, no rewarded doctor. The symptoms wax and wane in the face of various and relatively ineffective treatments. The patient needs his doctor, but he cannot please the doctor with a return to comfort and productivity. This is not an easy relationship, obviously, and professionals who are willing and able to give of themselves in such situations are both dedicated and uncommon.

In personally dealing with any illness, acute or chronic, realize that being sick is not a cut-and-dried matter. In reality, your health is a fluid, changing condition, a constantly shifting psychobiologic mosaic that can improve, deteriorate, or remain the same on a day-to-day, hour-to-hour, or even moment-to-moment basis.

Here are three self-administered comfort-productivity scales that can demonstrate how even severe chronic illness may be less debilitating than we think. They also provide an insightful and valuable measure of improvement on a day-to-day or week-to-week basis.

COMFORT-PRODUCTIVITY SCALES

In defining *comfort,* use your own judgment. In general, use some average of the amount of emotional and physical comfort you recall experiencing during the time periods listed below. Rely on all of your experience in arriving at your answer, both personal experience and what you have learned about the comfort levels of others.

In rating your comfort, use these guidelines: Optimal comfort (the most comfortable you have ever been) is 100. Use proportionate fractions of 100 for the amount of comfort that applies to you. If you feel your comfort is optimal for you, write down 100. If you feel your level of comfort is half of that which you would like to experience, write down 50. Zero, of course, means you are experiencing no comfort at all. Use any proportionate fraction of 100 that applies to you.

Optimal=100
My rating now ________
My rating for the past six months ________
What I would like my rating to be ________
What I would settle for ________

Productivity is defined as the ability to do the physical things that you want to do. For some that may mean working at hard physical tasks; for others, taking care of minimal bodily needs and personal wants. Use the definition that is appropriate for you. For example, a score of 100 may represent eight hours of hard physical work, for some; the ability to dress themselves, for others.

In rating your productivity, use these guidelines: Optimal productivity (the most productive you have ever been) is 100. Use proportionate fractions of 100 for the amount of productivity that applies to you. If you feel your productivity is optimal for you, write down 100. If you feel your level of productivity is half that which you would like, write down 50. If you feel you are wholly unproductive, write down 0. Use any proportionate fraction of 100 that applies to you.

Optimal=100
My rating now ____________
My rating for the past six months ____________
What I would like my rating to be ____________
What I would settle for ____________

Discomfort is defined as the presence of disabling symptoms, such as pain or shortness of breath, and the presence of disabling feelings, such as depression or fright.

In rating your discomfort, use these guidelines: The most severe discomfort you have ever experienced is assigned 100. Rank your discomfort level some number from 0 to 100. If your current level of discomfort is half the most severe you've ever experienced, write down 50. If you have no discomfort write down 0. Use any figure between 100 and 0 that applies to you.

Worst discomfort ever experienced=100
My rating now ____________
My rating for the past six months ____________
What I would like my rating to be ____________
What I would settle for ____________

Employing the comfort-productivity scales as a measure of illness, it's interesting to reconsider some of our popular ideas about sickness. Psoriasis, for example, the chronic, recurrent skin rash that, according to one television advertisement, is a disease accompanied by "lonely heartbreak." It's probable the average psoriasis patient feels more annoyed or irritated than heartbroken, but more important, the psoriasis patient may find he or she isn't badly off in the grand scheme of things. Such a person's productivity-comfort profile might look like this:

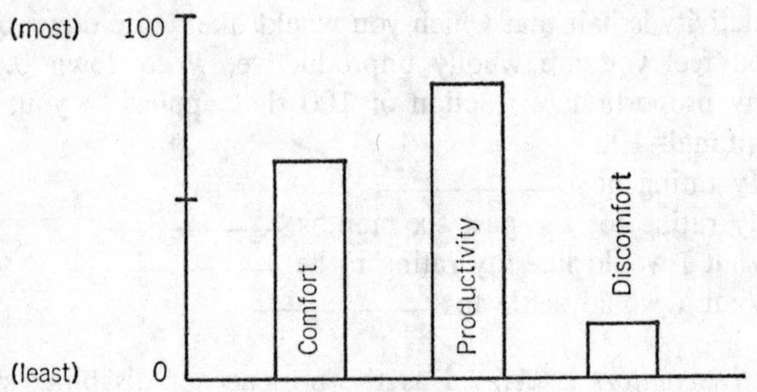

This is intriguing, because an Olympic marathon runner, in the home stretch, winning his race, might have a comfort-productivity profile resembling this:

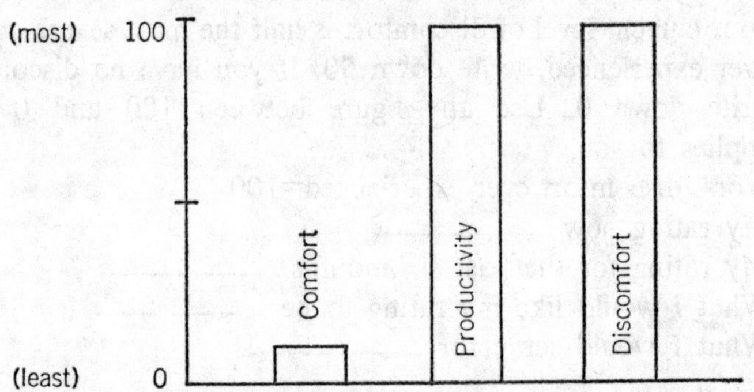

A congenitally deaf child, upon learning she is at last able to speak words her mother can understand and respond to, very likely has a comfort-productivity profile akin to this:

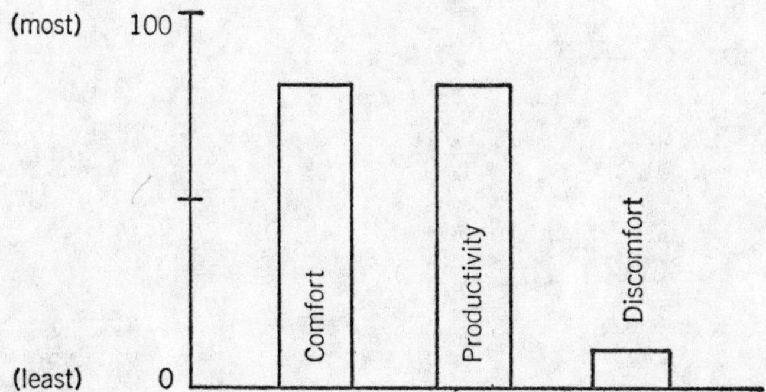

The comfort-productivity profile of a perfectly "healthy" corporate executive who is two hours behind schedule and stacked up over Chicago's O'Hare Airport in a stuffy commuter-jet might well look like this:

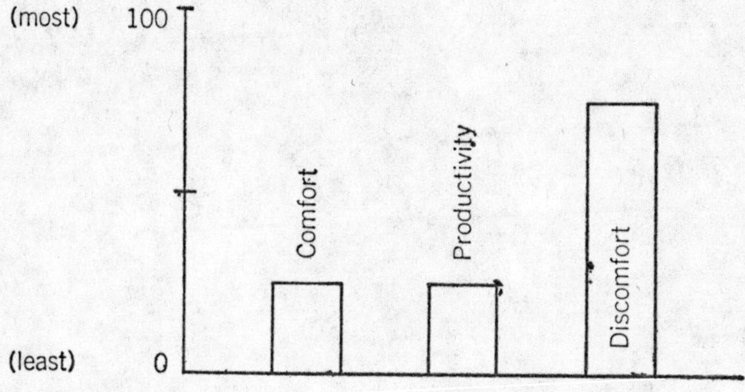

CHAPTER 10

WHEN YOUR BOSS GIVES YOU A HEADACHE

Approximately half the events listed on the Social Readjustment Scale involve dealing with other people. Receiving a traffic ticket, for example, or changing schools, or being fired, all place one in stressful situations involving others. It can be helpful to remember that *everyone* in such circumstances is subject to stress, not just you. The boss who must tell you he's letting you go may well be as upset by the encounter as you are. Law-enforcement experts point out that a policeman is seldom so vulnerable to armed assault as when he approaches a stranger in an automobile. In dealing with people it is always constructive to understand what the situation means to the other person. This can help ease tension for both of you. Especially in situations where you are in charge of, or advising someone else, you can ease potentially stressful circumstances by understanding what is being communicated to you. Since in any person-to-person transaction as much as 50 per cent of what is communicated is *non-verbal,* some knowledge of this non-verbal behavior is essential if you are going to deal with people in a systematic and reasonable manner.

All of us recognize some non-verbal clues. When meeting

people, we automatically notice their facial expressions, their body postures, and whether their speech is rapid or slow. We notice if they are angry or depressed. Few of us, however, do this in a systematic manner or use the information to benefit the interpersonal transaction. Still, the use of sophisticated non-verbal communication is easily within your grasp.

THE TELLTALE HANDSHAKE

When first meeting someone, notice how far the person stands from you and the temperature of his hand when you shake it. Hand temperature and body distance are important indicators of emotional expression in our culture.

Hand temperature tends to be cool or cold during three emotional states: anger, anxiety, and depression. Hand temperature increases to warm or hot during periods of resentment and during periods of comfort and contentment. Thus, by shaking someone's hand you can obtain a general idea as to whether he or she is more uncomfortable than you and perhaps some indication of how the person is feeling.

It is the *relative* difference in hand temperature compared to yours that is the key. Thus a hand slightly cooler than yours doesn't imply someone is acutely anxious in your presence, but rather that he or she would like to please you. In the same way, a hand somewhat warmer than yours doesn't mean the person resents you. More likely this person feels comfortable with you. When you encounter scalding or frigid handshakes, however, be alert for some volatile emotional states.

Suppose you are interviewing someone for a job with your company. Upon shaking hands with the applicant at the beginning of the interview, his hand is apt to be cooler than yours, an indication the applicant is anxious to please you. If the interview has been friendly and the applicant's hand is still cool at the conclusion of the interview, you know the applicant still wants to please you and does want the job. If the applicant's hand is now warmer than yours, the applicant may no longer be interested in the position.

The cool-warm hand relationship is a simple and reliable non-verbal cue; it can be an invaluable tool for a salesman in assessing the prospects he calls on. It will always be easier to make a sale to someone with cool hands, in relationship to yours, than someone with warm hands.

Similarly, a man seeking a sexual conquest will find it easier to seduce a partner with cold hands than with warm. For instance, contrary to appearances, it's seldom the flirtatious, warm-handed woman (the one surrounded by a phalanx of admiring men at a cocktail party) who is apt to accept the offer of a nightcap at your place or hers. Such a tryst is far more probable with the quiet, understated woman who has cold hands.

As a general rule, in loving and caring sexual interactions, a woman's hands will be cool in relation to a man's.

The distance someone stands from you while discussing matters is another index of emotional condition. In American society we normally hold people a "handshake" distance away, or the distance to reach out and shake someone's hand. Most people feel uncomfortable when anyone gets either closer than handshake distance or farther away. Thus handshake distance, or about three feet, is the optimum distance for good communication. If you know someone is feeling depressed or dependent, however, move in to stand or sit one or two feet away, because a depressed or dependent person is only acutely aware of space immediately around his or her body, and doesn't pay much attention to things that occur beyond that distance (reduced body space). On the other hand, if you notice that someone is shy, uncomfortable, hostile, or suspicious, he will be easier to communicate with if you stand or sit four to six feet away (expanded body space). Suspicious people have a body space that exceeds four feet. When someone approaches him closer than four or five feet, he feels the way you do when someone comes closer to you than three feet. In order to maintain good communication it may sometimes be necessary for you to establish a distance that isn't comfortable for you but is for the other person.

These kinds of observations are helpful in dealing with people, but they only scratch the surface of non-verbal clues.

THAT MAN GIVES ME A HEADACHE!

An illustration from what we've learned about psychophysiology points to another kind of non-verbal communication. We've all heard someone say "that man gives me a headache." This may be literally true. As described earlier, a tension headache occurs when there is sustained contraction of skeletal musculature of the head or neck. Muscle which contracts continuously shuts off its own blood supply, and with insufficient blood to supply its own metabolic needs, the muscle hurts. In general, this kind of headache is absent in the morning and increases in intensity as the day's tensions increase. This occurs because the skeletal musculature in the head and neck undergoes increasing contractions in many people as they become more tense and apprehensive. If someone you work with is susceptible to such tension headaches, it is useful to understand the relationship between emotional pressure, tension, apprehension, and head or neck pain. The more emotional pressure the more pain.

If your role is that of employer and you are giving your employee tension headaches, then you are reducing that employee's productivity. Differently, if you conduct yourself with that employee in such a way as to make the employee feel comfortable and trusting in your presence, you'll have a more productive employee. In some ways this represents a form of conditioning; you can condition the employee to feel comfortable in your presence or you can condition the employee to develop headaches in your presence. Too few supervisors understand this, indeed few corporation presidents understand this, and the subsequent loss in productivity to business and industry is staggering as a result.

Who wants to work hard for someone who gives him a headache?

If you are the headache-prone employee, you have basically three courses of action. You can convince your boss that she or he is making you tense and anxious, thus changing the boss's method of communicating with you. Or you can work at examining and changing your reaction to your boss. If both these solutions fail, it may well be best to quit and find a more comfortable job.

If all examples of non-verbal communication were as simple as tension headaches, it wouldn't pose much of a problem. Non-verbal communication is considerably more complex than headaches, however, and it involves some detailed examination of human behavior, attitudes, and disease. Just as a disease can be a coping mechanism, it can also represent non-verbal communication. In reality, the terms "coping behavior" and "non-verbal communication" are often two ways of saying the same thing.

ATTITUDES AND DISEASE

For years, scientists have attempted to associate various diseases with specific personality types, largely with inconclusive results. Another type of association has been increasingly successful, however, the association of specific attitudes with specific disease states. An attitude is defined as the way one feels about his illness and what he wishes he could do about it. Although people with the same disease may feel different emotionally (one may be depressed, one may be angry, one may be anxious) and may have different personality traits (one may be compulsive, another may be hypomanic) their attitudes toward their disease remain relatively constant. Because of this consistency, these attitudes are very useful in diagnosing disease. But the importance of these attitudes lies not only in what they tell you about the individual, but also what to avoid. A review of some diseases we've already explored serves to illustrate this.

The person who gets migraine headaches operates on a "stop-go" basis. He or she has a life oriented to being extremely active and busy or doing nothing. The migraines occur after a rapid transition has been made from a state of hyperactivity to inactivity. Once you understand this, the migraine becomes a non-verbal clue. The migraine is saying stop conducting business in a manner which increases hyperactivity during working hours and leads to increasing relaxation after working hours. If you get the migraines, the solution is obvious. If it's an employee of yours, some counseling is in order.

The person with low back pain has an intense need to get out or run away. Anything that increases this need to get away will increase the intensity of the back pain. Low-back-pain sufferers will go to considerable effort to remove themselves from situations or people that increase their discomfort. These are among the few people who will actually stand up and leave a formal interview if you make them uncomfortable. The pain apparently increases if you, the interviewer, increase the level of activation for the incipient low-back-pain sufferer.

Whenever anyone feels like running away or leaving a situation, there is a contraction of the muscle system in general; this is especially true of the back musculature which plays such an important part in holding the body erect while running. Once again, sustained muscle contraction decreases the blood flow to that muscle. With a decrease in blood flow, there is a decrease in the body's ability to remove metabolic waste from the muscle and to supply fresh oxygen. The result is pain. Thus, the simple expedient of making someone uncomfortable, tense, and feeling like running away can initiate a backache.

People with peptic ulcers generally feel deprived of things that they justly deserve. This feeling of deprivation can be very intense and can seriously obstruct communication. Again, this is a feeling which increases with increasing activity. As someone becomes more uncomfortable and activated, more stomach acid and enzymes are secreted, which produces increased stomach pain.

It is critical to recognize that people with peptic ulcer, backache and other common diseases are different from migraine headache patients. For example, giving a migraine patient an appointment or planning a business session after regular working hours may actually decrease the intensity and frequency of migraines. Thus, business may be easier to transact. On the other hand, people with duodenal ulcers or backache may have an increase in frequency and intensity of pain when given additional working responsibilities after hours.

Asthma is a complex disease, because it has two components. The asthmatic, during acute episodes, usually feels shut out and isolated by other people. Because of this, the asthmatic feels helpless; that is, having a condition for which he can't help himself, but that others can help. Such attacks normally occur in a setting of increased activation during which the person feels increasingly helpless and isolated. Unfortunately, the asthmatic tends to swing too far in both directions—like a migraine patient. After the attack an asthmatic tends to go into a period of inactivation. Instead of a headache, however, the asthma victim usually gets an infection.[1] This infection, most often pulmonary, appears then to be associated with increasing activation and another asthma attack, which in turn, is followed by a period of inactivation, ad infinitum. This isn't the easiest problem to deal with, but in a business climate being supportive and reassuring will help maintain a close and confident relationship and help decrease attacks.

People with diabetes mellitus feel as though they are starving in the midst of plenty. They have access to all the things that could be used to make them comfortable and life a suc-

[1] There is evidence that similar swings from activation to inactivation sometimes precipitate common colds. Students, for example, frequently come down with colds immediately after finishing final examinations.

cess, but for some reason they are unable to reach out and take advantage of them. Obviously then, you don't want to do anything to further increase a diabetic's feeling of alienation. Arranging business and social procedures to make a diabetic feel he is getting what he wants and needs will not only increase his ability to conduct business and function socially, but will also tend to bring the diabetes under better control.

People with high blood pressure feel threatened by something they cannot define. They feel they have to be constantly prepared for some kind of threat. In dealing with this type of individual, it is important to structure business and pleasure so that everything is understood well in advance and there is no unknown factor to make him feel unduly threatened.

People with hives generally feel beaten and subdued, as though something has been done to them and they have been unable to take any kind of constructive action. They have been beaten down and have had to take it "without striking back." They are easily resentful and frustrated and demand a considerable amount of your time and attention.

People with Raynaud's disease feel that something must be done. The something that must be done is usually destructive, and they feel a need to strike out and hurt others. In dealing with someone like this, it is advisable to use standard business and social practices which cannot be attacked at some later date. It is also wise to explain things in great detail.

The foregoing examples offer insight into the problems that people with some common diseases have. The information doesn't mean that every person you meet with asthma will tell you that he feels shut out in the cold, or that every person with migraine will say that things are over, finished, and done with. However, these are the general attitudes people adopt when they are experiencing these particular diseases. In dealing with them, you can view these different formulations as non-verbal cues and alter your behavior accordingly. Also, if you experience one of these diseases, the information may aid you in orienting your own life.

In the ordinary transactions of life, the more you know about people, the more comfortable and happy you will be, and the more comfortable and happy those around you will be. This kind of information contributes not only to your security in dealing with others, but it also adds considerable interest to interpersonal transactions that can make life richer and more meaningful.

Our best writers use non-verbal communication directly and indirectly; a master among them is Katherine Anne Porter. In these passages from her novel *Ship of Fools,* which is set in 1931, the cruise ship's Dr. Schumann is watching passengers board in Veracruz:

> . . . a tall boy with glittering golden hair and a sulky mouth pushed and jostled a light wheel chair along, in which sat a small weary dying man with weak dark whiskers flecked with gray, his spread hands limp on the brown rug over his knees, eyes closed. His head rolled gently with the movement of the chair, otherwise he gave no sign of life.
>
> A young Mexican woman, softened and dispirited by recent childbirth, dressed in the elegant, perpetual mourning of her caste, came up slowly, leaning on the arm of the Indian nurse who carried the baby, his long embroidered robe streaming over her arm almost to the ground. The Indian woman wore brightly jeweled earrings, and beneath her full, gaily embroidered Pueblo skirt her small bare feet advanced and retreated modestly . . .
>
> . . . The four pretty, slatternly Spanish girls, their dark hair sleeked down over their ears, thin-soled black slippers too short in the toes and badly run over at high heels, took leisurely leave, with kisses all around, of a half dozen local young men, who had brought flowers and baskets of fruit. Their own set of four wasp-waisted young men then joined them, and they strolled up together, the girls casting glances full of speculation at the row of fair-haired young officers . . .

> . . . An assortment of North Americans, with almost no distinguishing features that Dr. Schumann could see, except that they could not be other than Americans, came next. They were generally thinner and lighter-boned than the Germans, but not so graceful as the Spaniards and Mexicans.

Merely by offhand but practiced observations, the fictional Dr. Schumann systematically tells us a great deal about these people: nationality, taste, culture, and social background, along with clues about their personalities, moods, and circumstances. In a similar fashion, study your cohorts the next time you find yourself delayed in an airport boarding area. The nervous man in wing-tip shoes who keeps looking at his watch is probably a salesman with an important meeting at the other end of the flight. The young woman who re-examines her makeup every few minutes is going to be met upon landing by a husband or lover. The young man in casual dress, whose sideburns are closely trimmed above the ears, is on leave from the military, probably headed home from boot camp. The stylish fellow in conversation with the smiling stewardess will probably not dine alone this evening. The frail woman fidgeting with her asthma nebulizer is obviously apprehensive about the flight.

COMMUNICATING TO YOURSELF

Since we consciously think with language, some of our communication with ourselves is verbal; however, most of it isn't. We react to heat whether we "think" it's hot or not, just as we react to cold, hunger, happiness, fright, pain, an undulating ship's deck, a skittering skateboard, or a personal affront. When you leave shelter on a cold day, you do not verbally tell your body to adjust to chill, but as a psychobiologic unit you tell your body to adjust to the cold. You communicate to yourself non-verbally.

When a child ups and whacks his brother, the insulted sibling doesn't usually "think" about his response. He simply retaliates by slugging the offending brother right back. Only when asked why he hit his brother does the wronged child rationalize that "he hit me first." At the moment of assault he was mainly responding with non-verbalized anger. In New York City this kind of drama occurs ten thousand times a day, the taxicab horn may be our purest form of non-verbalized communication (the dialogue that often follows may be our impurest!)

It's probably safe to say that more words are written and thoughts are thought about human sexuality than other facets of life, but sexual stirrings and sexual intercourse are non-verbal modes of communication. The words, groans, and shrieks so celebrated by our pornography industry may sometimes accompany interpersonal sex, and so may a host of thoughts and fantasies—but there is nothing linguistic about sexual orgasm.

Learning to understand what you are communicating to yourself may be vastly more important to your health than sex, histrionics, or honking horns.

Let's suppose you dislike public speaking, actually dread public speaking, because it makes you miserably uncomfortable. For hours, even days, before you must address a large audience your stomach is in knots, you perspire for no apparent reason, you feel a shortness of breath. As the terrifying hour approaches, your discomfort increases. You feel numb, restless, frightened. Then there you are on the fateful day.

"And now ladies and gentlemen, I'm very pleased to introduce . . ." says the chairman. Your heart is cannonading, your hands are trembling, your throat aches, you wish you could simply die and end it all. But you press on, you persevere, you manage to rise and begin reading your speech, in a voice you don't recognize, to an audience you can't see through blurred eyes. Yet somehow you muddle through.

In our culture, muddling through is expected of us. Those among us who are terrified of flying in airplanes, or frightened of swimming, or intimidated by crowds are expected, from early childhood, to "grow up," to "bite the bullet," to "get a grip" on ourselves. Since our society admires these feats of overcoming anxiety, most of us do "tough it out," and the subsequent jolts to our systems we recognize as discomfort; sometimes severe discomfort. But we try, and we somehow hang on.

Despite popular opinion, why should anyone who reacts with severe stress to public speaking force himself to accept a public speaking invitation? To be sure, in a job in which public speaking is expected of you, you might seek professional counseling to help you overcome your problem. But to "tough out" such events on a regular basis, whether part of your job or not, is nothing more than a sure way to make yourself sick. If you can learn to stop reacting with stress to public speaking, that's one thing. It's certainly worth some effort to do so.[2] But if you cannot overcome your phobia, avoid public speaking. Continuing to engage in an activity that is overtly and continuously distressing to you makes as much sense as forsaking sleep or giving up food.

This doesn't mean you should avoid everything that might make you feel uneasy. Often the anticipation of an event will cause some discomfort, or even considerable discomfort. The extraordinary Fred Biletnikoff, a brilliant pass receiver for the Oakland Raiders, sometimes vomits in the locker room just before game time. Yet his performance on the field appears as close to flawless as can be accomplished in the tumultuous game of professional football. Inevitably, a sprinter feels ill at ease before the gun goes off for an important track race. It's natural for an actress to have opening-night butterflies before the curtain rises. But when the curtain rises, she becomes the professional she is. When the gun fires, the sprinter takes off with practiced, fluid strides. And when Biletnikoff patterns

[2] According to Hans Selye, antiadrenaline drugs may help. They can overcome many of the distressing aspects of public speaking without interfering with a speaker's presentation.

downfield among quick and nasty defensive linebackers, he moves with inspired confidence.

There is, however, a considerable difference between some nervousness preceding a great performance and clutching your seat for the duration of a two-hour airplane flight, or feeling panic in a crowded room, or experiencing terror every time you enter an elevator. *In essence, these kinds of stress reactions represent your effort to communicate non-verbally with you.* You are saying to yourself, "I shouldn't be here because this isn't good for me."

Listen!

CHAPTER 11

SURVIVAL IN THE REAL WORLD

> In a world-wide war of movement, you may suddenly find yourself stranded in unfamiliar conditions and surroundings in the Arctic, on the ocean, on a coral island, or in the jungle, or desert. You may tend to magnify the hazards of these strange places because of this unfamiliarity. Fear of the unknown weakens you by reducing your ability to think and plan. If you are armed with knowledge acquired beforehand, no part of the world will be completely strange or frightening to you. You will be capable of coping with the new surroundings and returning to your base in good physical and mental trim.
>
> —*How to Survive on Land and Sea,*
> U. S. Naval Institute, 1943

Survival in the real world depends upon your ability to cope —just as it did on a coral reef in the Pacific in 1943, and just as it always has and always will. And as the World War II training manual stressed, *acquired knowledge* is the essence of coping.

The ability to cope with life is related to many factors, not least among them your family background; however, coping ability is not directly linked to the amount of money, longevity, success, or happiness your family had before you. Coping depends on what you *learned* about the factors that contributed to successes before you and/or successes around you. It's possible that if you were born with a million dollars in the bank you will do better in life than if you were born with nothing. Yet a millionaire from birth may lose everything if coping ability—the essential ingredient to successful life management—isn't present in his personality.

Differently, in Horatio Alger tradition, anyone raised in a lower-class ghetto has about the same chance to learn successful coping as someone raised with a "silver spoon" in his mouth.[1] Actually, a tough ghetto is as good or better a place to learn successful coping than most environments. Because a major component of coping is learning how to deal with many different complex and difficult situations in an adaptive manner and not be overwhelmed by them, a ghetto world can be an excellent teacher. The advantage and disadvantage of a ghetto is that it is capable of variously producing the best and worst of conditions in terms of learning the ability to cope. To be sure, the unending problems and confrontations of ghetto life overwhelm and crush many, who simply give up. This is the relentless tragedy of ghettos. Still, for those who rise to meet ghetto challenges, who learn they can fight the odds and win, the ultimate in personalities able to cope may well develop. Witness the great jazz musician Louis Armstrong, Congresswoman Shirley Chisholm, or Kenneth Allen Gibson, the self-confident and articulate Newark mayor who rose to power from the ghetto of his city's central ward.[2]

In contrast, growing up within a rich and successful family

[1] Making a million dollars doesn't represent successful coping, in fact, or in the often misinterpreted Horatio Alger tradition. No one in a Horatio Alger book became a millionaire, a fact noted in *The Dictionary of Misinformation:* "Alger heroes were bootblacks and newsboys. They persevered with great virtue. They paid off mortgages, and they achieved respectability. But in monetary terms their success was modest—with perhaps a raise from $5 to $10 per week."

[2] Mayor Gibson was among the first black, big-city mayors in the United States. He "never bucked the system," George Metcalf writes, "but chose instead to work from within and make it work."

may not be the enviable experience most of us imagine. In terms of development, some people require the kinds of daily challenges found only in difficult living conditions in order to develop their abilities to cope. Otherwise they never learn, and sooner or later they simply fail to adapt.

Another component and fact of life about coping is that some people who cannot cope survive because of their supportive families, or because of the "silver spoons" they were born with. These are vulnerable individuals, however, for should their money, influence, or support crumble, their difficulties in dealing with life will overtake them. Their counterparts are those who enjoy unlimited coping resilience, people who may never be "wealthy, esteemed, or accomplished," and yet who live comfortable, rich, and productive lives.

For the fortunate who combine constructive and successful family background with a high degree of coping ability, success and survival are virtually assured. Scions of John David Rockefeller are perhaps our society's salient examples, but there are others. Nevertheless, whatever one's background—rich, poor, stimulating, somber, orderly, or a shambles—*an ability to cope is the overriding condition of success and survival.*

It's also important to know that success, failure, and survival are relative to the world we live in. Personal goals must be realistic. Someone with extraordinary coping abilities will fail in an attempt to become dictator of the United States. Goals always need to be tempered with judgment and the realization that a particular goal may be unobtainable at the time desired. People who are best at coping know this and accept it; they know how to accept alternative goals or parallel goals.

A man who would be king will fail if he cannot accept an alternative to being king. A man stranded on a coral reef will fail if he cannot cope with the reality of finding himself on a coral reef.

The following case histories demonstrate various degrees of coping ability and its relationship to recovering from illness. We present them to help you step back and look at yourself and your relative place in the world. These brief summaries, though not always optimistic, can help all of us understand why people get into medical trouble, and how some are able to extricate themselves from trouble. Above all, these examples drawn from real life should serve to assure you that survival has little to do with starting at the bottom or the top. It's your present available coping ability that counts—and how you use it.

NANCY—HIGH LIFE CHANGE AND LOW COPING ABILITY

Nancy was a twenty-one-year-old who had developed a disease called systemic lupus erythematosus at age thirteen. She had always enjoyed good health up to that point. But at thirteen she encountered peer-group competition for the first time, and she felt she could not compete as well as the other girls, despite the fact she was intelligent and attractive. She sensed that she was not as good at coping as those she was competing with and responded by feeling beaten and overwhelmed. Soon she also began to feel guilty for not living up to her potential. It was at that point that she developed symptoms, a butterfly rash on her face, swollen painful joints, and kidney disease. The disease progressed rapidly despite medical treatment.

At age sixteen Nancy was elected editor of her school's magazine, and the disease abated. As editor of the magazine she had no signs or symptoms of the disease, what's more she did not feel guilty or overwhelmed. In fact, she felt euphoric and actively competitive. Following graduation from high school, at age seventeen, she started college. The feelings of guilt and depression returned and so did the symptoms and signs of lupus erythematosus. Again, she reported that the disease flared up in a setting in which she felt beaten and overwhelmed. The disease continued to progress, despite intensive medical care.

At age twenty, when she was a college junior, Nancy became pregnant, the result of a fleeting love affair. She felt terribly guilty; she sought and soon found an admirer who was willing to marry her. However, when her pregnancy became apparent and the date of conception obvious, she felt hopeless, beaten, and unable to cope with life in any way. Her depression was bitterly aggravated by the opinions of some relatives who told her the disease was just retribution for her being "sinful." Nancy became inundated by guilt and deliberately cut herself in order to feel pain which she said punished her and took away some of the intense guilt.

In this setting of feeling guilty, depressed, and unable to cope, she developed irreversible kidney and heart failure. She died six months following the delivery of a normal, healthy boy, despite every possible effort to save her at one of the world's excellent medical centers.

MARY—HIGH LIFE CHANGE AND HIGH COPING ABILITY

Mary was an eighteen-year-old high school senior who had been raised in a happy family. She enjoyed great success in school, and indeed her entire family took pride in academic achievement. Both parents were physicians. Mary was the youngest of their four children; her brothers and sister had all completed college and were well along in graduate school and careers.

Mary's father had recently taken flying lessons, qualifying for a single-engine license. Her older brothers and sister strongly objected to this because, as they said, their father had recently developed high blood pressure; what's more, he was embroiled in a nuisance malpractice suit filed against him by a paranoid patient. The suit was groundless but unsettling, and the children were nervous about their father taking up flying during such an emotionally trying time.

They were right.

On a flight with his wife from western Washington to eastern Washington, their father's plane crashed in the rugged Snoqualmie Pass region of the Cascade Mountains. Both parents were killed upon impact.

The children were nearly inconsolable. They felt responsible and helpless, as if they should have been able to exert more control over their parents. They felt they could have averted the tragedy but didn't.

Mary was the most affected. She felt lonely, isolated, and depressed. In the months following her parents' deaths she became irritable and unco-operative. In this setting she experienced asthma for the first time, a severe attack that required hospitalization and treatment in an intensive care unit. Mary's siblings rallied around her, reminding her of her ability to work out problems. They urged her not to give up. They pointed out her own high standards of performance. This led to a family conference in which all four children agreed to work together in a way helpful to them to solve their individual reactions to their parents' deaths. Mary was included in all these deliberations; she felt supported and that her brothers and sister were working together constructively. In this setting the asthma remitted completely.

Today, six years after the death of Mary's parents, she is a successful medical student with excellent prospects ahead. She has had no recurrence of the asthma, and she has maintained an active, confident approach to life.

JACK—HIGH LIFE CHANGE AND AVERAGE COPING ABILITY

Jack was twenty-two years old when he was medically evacuated from Vietnam and admitted to a military psychiatric ward for an acute situational reaction to combat.[3] He served four years in the Marines with two tours of duty in Vietnam. He came from an intact middle-class family with a successful

[3] An acute situational reaction is a mental collapse in the face of overwhelming problems, which is reversible when the problems are removed.

father, mother, and sister. All family members were living and well. He was an outgoing, popular student in high school, who had spent a comfortable six months in college before joining the military. There was no history of difficulty with authority or disciplinary problems at home.

His difficulties began after suffering bayonet wounds in the face and chest while engaged in hand-to-hand combat in 1967. He was squad leader during this engagement, the sole survivor of the combat operation. He also experienced shrapnel wounds in February 1968 and again in March 1968.

Following the annihilation of his squad, Jack had repeated nightmares in which his squad was being killed and he was being bayoneted.

On returning to the United States, in late 1968, he was promoted and assigned to the position of drill instructor. Early in his new post, a recruit in his charge "insulted" him stating he was not going to serve in that "fucking immoral war" in Vietnam. Jack savagely assaulted the recruit, severely beating him. Jack was subsequently reduced in rank.

Following this incident Jack volunteered to return to Vietnam, to "get even." Back in Asia his nightmares recurred, and he was continually jumpy and anxious. He often awoke at night, waving a loaded automatic weapon, yelling and screaming, and then had no recollection of the episode the following day.

After another medical screening, he was again returned to the United States, hospitalized, treated, and returned to full duty with the exception that he was disqualified for assignment in Vietnam.

He served his remaining period of enlistment without incident and returned to a comfortable, productive civilian life.

JOEL—HIGH LIFE CHANGE AND LOW COPING ABILITY

Accidents are extraordinary phenomena which receive modest attention and seem to be accepted as a way of life in America, yet they are the major source of death in the one-to-thirty-five-year-old group. A disease with a mortality this high normally attracts the best of scientific minds and gargantuan grants of money. Studies of accidents rarely attract either.

Roughly 112,000 Americans were killed and another 10,800,000 experienced disabling injuries from accidents in 1967, a typical year. In the unpopular Vietnam War, total American combat deaths from January 1961 to October 1968 were approximately 29,034, with another 182,135 non-fatal wounds. These kinds of figures aroused great public anguish in the late sixties. However, our young men were more likely to be killed or injured on our highways than they were to be killed or injured in Vietnam in 1967, just as they are today.

An example of how such accidents occur is provided by Joel, a twenty-year-old divorced male with a high school education. He was an average student in high school who had difficulty coping with work and people. He started drinking alcoholic beverages at age fifteen. During high school he worked after school in order to buy a car. At this time he experienced increasing problems with his parents and used the car to work off his anger at them. In his words, "I would take a nice long ride to cool off." His nice long rides were episodes of fast, competitive, and reckless highway driving. During altercations with his parents he "wanted to haul off and hit someone" and he "wanted to scream." Most of these arguments were related to his use of alcohol and reckless driving.

Sometimes, while driving late at night, Joel thought he saw someone run in front of his car. He would scream and stop the automobile, only to find no one there.

About the time of his graduation from high school he was

diagnosed as having a peptic ulcer and polycythemia vera (a familial blood disease), both of which were treated with fair control.

After high school he worked in a supermarket briefly, quit because of personality problems, and then went to work in a paper mill.

One year after graduation, while drunk, he destroyed a new car in an automobile accident but survived. Two years after graduation, again drunk, he repeated the performance.

Shortly after this second accident Joel married a girl following a week's courtship. The marriage went poorly and his wife moved in with another man four months later. Following her departure, Joel took to drinking heavily, as "relief" from anxiety and "escape" from reality. He characterized this period of his life as feeling like "someone had taken me and torn me in two." Approximately one month after his marital separation, Joel "accidently" ran his car into a bridge. He received multiple fractures and other injuries including a laceration of his heart. He required open-heart surgery on three occasions, and a total of ten hospitalizations and multiple corrective operations in the five years following this accident, all a direct result of the accident.

In the year prior to his last accident, Joel had accumulated over seven hundred life-change units, placing him in an extremely high-risk category. Coupled with his habit of using automobiles and alcohol to discharge anger, this would lead one to think that his crippling accident, suffering, and staggering accompanying expense were predictable and probably preventable.

ANNE—HIGH LIFE CHANGE AND HIGH COPING ABILITY

Anne had started teaching at age twenty and continued on a full-time basis until she was eighty. She came from a hard-working family who were also loving and enjoyed themselves.

Her memories of childhood were pleasant and comfortable. As an adult she said it was fun to be alive and to be able to actively contribute what she could. As a teacher she was productive, loved, and capable. Upon turning eighty she continued to work as a "substitute" teacher, but in reality often worked about as many hours as she had at age fifty. She was bright, active, and alive. However, she had not reached the age of eighty without some hardship and turmoil.

The last serious period of travail in her life occurred when she was seventy-two. At that time she had her husband, three grown children, eight grandchildren, and two great-grandchildren. Her favorite grandchild, a beautiful, bright, but unstable young woman who recently had given birth to a child of her own, experienced a severe post partum depression and killed herself by running her car into a bridge abutment.

Anne was heartbroken and fell into deep depression. Her deceased granddaughter's husband found that he was unable to care for the baby, because of his own depression, and he left the child with Anne. In this setting, Anne's husband of fifty years died, increasing her anguish. Shortly thereafter Anne developed a severe cramping pain in her abdomen. An X ray revealed a carcinoma of the large bowel.

Anne was determined to overcome all difficulties and to continue living. She was adamantly against any solution that required taking her great-grandchild away from her or the child's father. They would come through as a family. On her own she decided the first thing she would have to deal with was her depression. She consulted a psychiatrist who felt she needed immediate surgery, but agreed with her that with her level of depression, surviving surgery was unlikely. She was treated with antidepressant medications and supportive psychotherapy. She responded rapidly to treatment and within two weeks felt that she was ready to undertake the surgery.

She made a deal with the surgeon. She felt that she could not continue her life with a colostomy, and he agreed to do a bowel resection instead, regardless of the amount of carcinoma present.[4] Fortunately the carcinoma was localized and the diseased portion of the bowel was removable. Following surgery Anne recovered rapidly and was back caring for her great-grandchild and grandson-in-law within four weeks. Everyone was amazed at her energy and ability to recuperate.

She rapidly put her life back together and emotionally supported her grandson-in-law until he was able to get back on his feet. During this period she loaned him a substantial amount of money to get his business restarted. After observing her ability and willingness to cope with adversity, he felt ashamed of himself and began to work hard to get the business going again. She encouraged him to start dating, and he remarried a year or so later.

At this point Anne felt that she "had a new lease on life," went back to teaching, and has been active and comfortable since. She takes care of herself, continues to live in the original family home, and is independent of her family for care or support. She has arranged matters so that in case of an emergency she is to be placed in a "retirement home" which has a nursing unit. She continues to insist upon the dignity and control of her life that has characterized her for eighty years.

DAVE—HIGH LIFE CHANGE AND LOW COPING ABILITY

Dave was eighteen years old with eleven months of active duty in the military when he was admitted to a military psychiatric ward with a diagnosis of a permanent inability to cope with life. He was removed from Vietnam early in his first tour of duty there.

He came from a severely disrupted family. Dave's father divorced his mother when Dave was one year of age. He lived with the mother who married a homosexual the following year. The homosexual stepfather brutally abused Dave, two

[4] A colostomy is a surgical hole in the abdominal wall which allows waste materials from the bowel to be rerouted from the rectum. It is employed when there is disease too severe for continued normal function of the rectum.

older brothers, and a younger sister. About the time Dave was seven, the stepfather began fondling the children's genital organs and shortly thereafter engaged in fellatio with the patient and his brothers; sexual intercourse with the sister. When Dave and his sister complained to their mother and attempted to disengage from the sexual practices of the stepfather, they were severely beaten, reprimanded, and further sexually abused.

When Dave and his sister were approximately seventeen years of age, the stepfather's behavior came to the attention of the police. He was arrested and Dave was sent to a military induction center to get him away from his home situation and to "make a man of him."

Dave was unable to complete high school courses, dropping out at the ninth-grade level. He experienced extreme anxiety when faced with dominant male figures or with females whether they were dominant or not. He was immature and dependent.

During his short time in the military he was unable to tolerate aggressive behavior in others. He had increasingly severe feelings of anxiety and fright when confronted with aggression. This was particularly true when confronted with the need to fight in combat. After the loss of two friends in combat, Dave was unable to tolerate being near combat zones although he had never been in combat himself. When evacuated to the United States he was unable to eat, unable to sleep, could not think coherently, and was twenty pounds below his normal weight.

He was treated with medications, behavioral therapy, and psychotherapy, and he recovered. It was evident, however, that he would not be able to cope with the military in any way, and he was subsequently given an honorable discharge without the need to fulfill his tour of duty.

JOAN—HIGH LIFE CHANGE AND HIGH COPING ABILITY

Joan, a thirty-eight-year-old advertising executive, came from a working-class family in which her father and mother both held down full-time jobs to make ends meet. She was the second of three children. The parents coped well with life and taught their children all they knew. It was a loving but realistic family in which the children were expected to be on their own after high school because of economic necessity. All three children understood the need to support themselves and contribute their share to the family finances.

Joan had been very successful. Her earnings exceeded those of her husband, who was the successful president of a small corporation. They had two children who were well, happy, and good students.

At about twenty-five, Joan noticed she had more energy than the rest of her family. Her need for sleep decreased to as little as four hours a night, and her ability to work and recreate increased. In this period she plunged into the advertising business, and quickly earned a national reputation. Yet despite her workload, she remained a devoted and loving mother and wife. This period of extraordinary energy lasted until she was thirty-one, when she experienced the first severe depression of her life.

Previously she had had modest "lows" which lasted several months and slowed her down, but did not incapacitate her. However, at age thirty-one the world caved in. She developed a severe, incapacitating retarded depression over a period of several weeks. She felt hopeless, the world was black, and she wanted to die. Her family mobilized all their efforts to console her and assure her she was needed and loved. Nothing helped. She was convinced of her worthlessness, and that she deserved to die. In this frame of mind she stabbed herself in the chest with a carving knife. She was rushed to an emergency hospital where she received interim treatment, and then was transferred to a large general hospital with facilities for open-heart surgery. She underwent corrective surgery for repair of a laceration of the heart, which fortunately was superficial.

Following surgery she was referred to psychiatry service where the diagnosis of manic-depressive illness was made.

Joan was at first skeptical and frightened of the medications and psychotherapy recommended for the management of her disease. She was bewildered as to how she could be so successful in life with such a serious psychiatric illness. After it was explained that people with manic-depressive disease tend to be more successful than the average population she felt more comfortable, but remained skeptical. She was initially treated with antidepressant medication and lithium carbonate. The depression cleared in two weeks, and she began to regain her former high energy level; her spirits became almost euphoric. During the next year she learned to effectively use lithium carbonate, antidepressant medications, and neuroleptics, and she adjusted rapidly to short-term psychotherapy.[5]

It was evident from the beginning of her therapy that she was bright, perceptive, and able to adjust to almost anything provided she was given adequate information to work with. By the end of one year she knew enough about her illness to treat it herself with some supportive therapy and advice from a psychiatrist every one to six months.

In the intervening seven years since the near-fatal stab wound, she has successfully raised her children to college age, further increased her income and status in the community, maintained a successful marriage, and, above all, has been happy and content with her life.

[5] Neuroleptics are the psychoactive medications used to treat major psychiatric diseases other than depression.

ROGER—HIGH LIFE CHANGE AND LOW COPING ABILITY

Roger, a twenty-year-old lance corporal in the Marines with three years of active duty, was admitted to the psychiatric support service from his combat unit in Vietnam and subsequently transferred to the United States for psychiatric observation and treatment. After observation for a period of several months, a diagnosis of chronic drug use in combination with depression and a personality disorder was made, and he was subsequently given an honorable discharge from the military.

Roger had a past history of depression and associated disciplinary problems. He became a chronic drug user about one year prior to his rotation to Vietnam, while in high school. He said that drugs reduced the intensity of his depression, and he was using an assortment of drugs on a regular basis.

In Vietnam he relied mainly on marijuana and opium. These placed him in a "dream world" in which he couldn't give or carry out orders. While serving as a corporal he was unable to give orders to his men or to lead them. He insisted on *requesting* that his men carry out his orders. When they did not, he would do the tasks himself. As a result, his control of his men in combat was loose and fragmented; several of his squad members were wounded in situations that were preventable. He simply did not have the energy or drive to take appropriate protective measures while in the field.

After serving his regular rotation in Vietnam, Roger extended. He stated it was because "I was just having a good time." He was "high most of the time" on opium. Approximately two months before his return to the United States, as a result of his poor combat record, he was screened, found to be in possession of marijuana, and reduced in rank from corporal to lance corporal. He was also sentenced to the brig for ninety days and fined two months' wages. After serving his time he immediately returned to using opium and was subsequently sent home for psychiatric evaluation.

His disciplinary problems had begun in high school where he was unable to adapt to rules or regulations and could not accept directions from anyone. At the age of fifteen he was expelled from school. He felt that school was a "waste of time" and then worked at a variety of odd jobs until age seventeen when he joined the Marines. He enlisted with the Marines to escape "hassles" with his parents, both of whom were well educated and successful. He thought that in the Marines he would be free to do what he wanted.

While he was in the psychiatric service his depression cleared without treatment. He had no regrets about the members of his squad who were wounded as a result of his inability to perform and stated that he would not take drugs while in the hospital but would return to them as soon as he was discharged.

He returned to a civilian life of conflict with authority, drug abuse, and continued inability to perform or succeed.

GEORGE—HIGH LIFE CHANGE AND HIGH COPING ABILITY

George was a forty-five-year-old president of a small corporation who had climbed the ladder of success all by himself. He had tremendous self-confidence, excellent social skills, intelligence, and an ability to cope with just about any problem. Still, during the frenetic period of business expansion, he began to feel overwhelmed and in need of a rest. With typical energy and enthusiasm, he arranged for a six-week vacation for himself and his family to an isolated region of Mexico.

George was going to spend his days reading and resting with an occasional fishing trip. His wife and two sons had an excursion itinerary that looked almost as hectic as George's typical schedule at home. After ten days of this idyllic, restful period in George's life he had a heart attack. The attack began while the family was away on a field trip, and there was no one nearby to aid him. A radio-telephone was on hand, however, and George managed to radio for a physician to fly in by plane.

By the time his family returned, he had assured his own rescue but was unconscious. He had dutifully left a note for the family just in case he died or was unconscious when they returned. Within a short while he was on a plane to a major medical center where he rapidly responded to treatment.

A month following his heart attack he returned to the United States feeling in good health and with a high energy level. He returned to his business and had no further difficulties with his heart in two subsequent years of medical follow-up.

In various ways, the foregoing case histories demonstrate what kinds of people survive and what kinds do not. As we've seen, high levels of life change are dangerous to everyone, but even when confronted with sad and terrible life changes, some among us refuse to feel helpless or hopeless. These people, like eighty-year-old Anne, cope with reality in the most positive and constructive way possible. Others, like twenty-year-old Joel, crumble under the stress of dealing with life changes. It is a cliché, but an accurate one, to say the essential difference between success and failure in life is a matter of attitude. Recall Dr. Richter's experimental rats described in Chapter 4? Tossed into water, one rat drowned in minutes; the other rat treaded water for days. One rat gave up easily. The other rat was determined to survive.

LONGEVITY

We know that health and longevity are the payoffs for coping with, and minimizing, the ravages of stress; yet in the United States there are only some three centenarians per 100,000 people, which makes the study of them difficult. In our country people over one hundred are a rare breed. In contrast, there are three isolated regions of the world where remarkable numbers of people live past one hundred years.

In 1970, 9 inhabitants among 819 in the Ecuadorian village of Vilcabamba were over 100, the senior being about 110. Statistically, Harvard's Jean Mayer points out, that's 1,100 centenarians per 100,000! Hunzaland, a remote valley in the Himalayas, also boasts a high proportion of centenarians, although accurate data aren't available. But well documented data is available from the Republic of Georgia in Russia, where there are 39 centenarians per 100,000; in neighboring Azerbaijan region, there are 84 per 100,000.

In examining the lives of residents in these three widely separated regions of the world, Dr. Mayer points to the fact that community hygiene doesn't seem to be a factor in longevity. In Hunzaland, anemia, goiter, tuberculosis, and pneumonia are commonplace, and almost everyone has intestinal worms.

Nor does diet seem to be significant. Some of the oldsters drink a great deal of wine and vodka, while others drink sparingly or not at all. Some eat mostly vegetables and fruits, while others eat a range of foods. Some maintain diets low in calories, proteins, and fats. Some eat proteins and fats in quantity. In the Caucasus Mountains of Russia, the elderly have intakes of proteins and calories that are about the same as that of Americans.

"Amazingly," says Dr. Mayer, "there are even a few obese centenarians."

Dr. Mayer doesn't draw conclusions from his observations, but he adds this:

"In all three cultures, the people are physically active. They are primarily farmers who labor by hand and walk rather than ride. There is no forced retirement; many hold jobs until they are 100 or older; their work is necessary, their advice is solicited, their wisdom respected."

Drawing from what we currently know about stress, it's fascinating to speculate about the lives of these centenarians. Their isolated communities have been little influenced by the world's political and social upheavals of the past century, and there has been little population movement in or out of the communities. Hence levels of life change for the residents of these three regions have probably been modest. What's more, the rhythms of living have not been marked by great highs or lows in activation. Births, burials, marriages, child rearing, planting, and harvesting have filled these lives. Quiet, solid activities not characterized by thrilling victories or agonizing defeats. And, perhaps most important of all, these lives have seldom been jolted by milestones, stopping points, or changes in direction–no ceremonial passages from childhood, adolescent honors and competitions, adult pursuit of promotions, changes in careers, or forced retirements. These have been lives, in other words, characterized by modest degrees of stress. Dull lives, perhaps, by the standards of our culture, but content lives nevertheless. To be respected and considered wise at age one hundred must certainly be a pleasure. And to work in the fields at one hundred must offer rich rewards. The thinning mists of another dawn, gentle breezes through the corn rows, the musical concerts of blackbirds as you walk the irrigation ditch . . . these may well mean more at age one hundred than any measure of wealth or fame at age fifty.

YOU ARE WHAT YOU EAT?

"You are what you eat" is a beloved saying among those concerned about nutrition. It's a fanciful image biochemically, but it does underscore the point that you have control over your health and well being. To repeat the theme of this book, in the day-to-day contest of surviving stress, life change, activation coastering, becoming sick, having an accident, or recovering from illness, you exert extraordinary control over your psychobiology and destiny.

Confronted with a heart attack in rural Mexico, George's reaction was to seek the best available solution to the problem. Confronted with pressures of high school, Roger's reaction

EPILOGUE

A CHECKLIST FOR SURVIVAL

In dealing with the problems of life, it is only human to seek simple answers. In that vein you may ask of this book, what's the punch line? What is the key, the panacea, the technique to this survival business?

For all the amazing information that has emerged from research into psychosocial medicine and psychophysiology in recent years, a quick and easy solution to the control of disease and disease symptoms has not been found. In questions of health and disease, simple answers do not occur. Still, throughout this book we have presented instructions and information to help the reader understand and control the complex stress-related mechanisms that are our major causes of illness.

From a current medical point of view, our approach is not fashionable. To be scientifically *au courant*, we would have to deal with every disease as though the only defect was biochemical or physiological, and thus ignore the multifaceted reality of disease. *Above all, we hope we have demonstrated that disease is not the simple result of simple causes, but rather the complex result of an infinite range of human ecological factors.*

In a sense, that is our punch line.

From the viewpoint of health and comfort, an ideal life would be one marked by absolute psychosocial and physiological stability, a life characterized by a willingness to be adequate to the tasks immediately ahead, no more and no less. In such a life there would be no looking back or reflection, nor would there be much interest in, or concern about, the future. One challenge and one solution at a time, without analysis or contemplation. Obviously, few of us would aspire to such a life-style, but the lesson to be learned from the illustration is that psychosocial stability is necessary to good health and comfort, while psychosocial instability is the prelude to disease and discomfort. Pacing your psychosocial and psychophysiologic well being is what this book is about. Though simplified, our message can be condensed into the following checklist for survival. If you take the time to think about what these suggestions mean on a day-to-day basis, they can be invaluable to your health and well being.

☐ Be aware that your emotional and physical health are one and the same.

☐ Avoid excessive life change, for too much life change produces stress and disease.

☐ Avoid great swings in activity levels; instead maintain a steady level of productive activity at work and play. Pace yourself.

☐ If you are uncomfortable, examine and consider changing your attitudes about life and your present circumstances. If you are ill, examine and consider your attitude about your illness.

☐ Remember that illness and discomfort are relative events, not absolute events. You are probably better off than you previously thought you were.

☐ Study those around you who appear to cope well with the problems of life, and mimic their coping behaviors if you can do so comfortably.

☐ Learn to understand what people are communicating to you non-verbally as well as verbally. Insight into the feelings of others can help minimize tensions in interpersonal transactions.

☐ Realize you are your own best physiological laboratory. Pay attention to how you react to events and circumstances. When you feel uncomfortable, try to alter your reaction and/or the situation.

☐ Never forget that your frame of mind can enormously influence your health, well being, and survival. The idea that a positive attitude is healthy is more than just a cliché–it can save your life.

BIBLIOGRAPHY

Chapter 1

Gunderson, E. K. E., and Rahe, R. H. *Life Stress and Illness.* Springfield, Ill.: Charles C Thomas, 1974.

Hinkle, L. E., Jr., and Wolff, H. G. "The nature of man's adaptation to his total environment and the relation of this to illness." *Archives of Internal Medicine* 99:442–60, 1957.

Holmes, T. H. "The Scholar and the Devil's Advocate." In *Report of the First Institute on Clinical Teaching.* Evanston, Ill.: Association of American Medical Colleges, 1959.

———, and Rahe, R. H. *Booklet for Schedule of Recent Experience (SRE).* Four-page questionnaire. Seattle: University of Washington, 1967.

———, and Rahe, R. H. "The Social Readjustment Rating Scale." *Journal of Psychosomatic Research* 11:213–18, 1967.

Rahe, R. H. "Life crisis and health change." In *Psychotropic Drug Response: Advances in Prediction.* P. R. A. May and J. R. Wittenborn (eds.). Springfield, Ill.: Charles C Thomas, 1969. Pp. 92–125.

Wolf, S., and Goodell, H. (eds.). *Harold G. Wolff's Stress and Disease,* revised, 2nd ed. Springfield, Ill.: Charles C Thomas, 1968.

Chapter 2

Blevins, W. *Give Your Heart to the Hawks.* Los Angeles: Nash, 1973.

Blythe, P. *Stress Disease.* New York: St. Martin's, 1973.

Cannon, W. B. *Bodily Changes in Pain, Hunger, Fear and Rage.* 2nd ed. New York and London: Appleton Co., 1929.

Chittenden, H. M. *The American Fur Trade of the Far West.* New York: Press of the Pioneers, 1935.

Dohrenwend, B., and Bruce P. (eds.). *Stressful Life Events.* New York: John Wiley & Sons, 1974.

Dubos, R. *Man Adapting.* New Haven and London: Yale University Press, 1965.

Gunderson, E. E. K., and Rahe, R. H. *Life Stress and Illness*. Springfield, Ill.: Charles C Thomas, 1974.

Hinkle, L. E. "The concept of 'stress' in the biological and social sciences." *Science Medicine and Man* 1:31–48, 1973.

James, T. *Three Years Among the Indians and Mexicans*. New York: Citadel, 1966.

McQuade, W., and Aikman, A. *Stress*. New York: E. P. Dutton, 1974.

Selye, H. *Stress Without Distress*. Philadelphia and New York: J. B. Lippincott Company, 1974.

——. *The Stress of Life*. New York: McGraw-Hill, 1976.

Tanner, O. *Stress*. New York: Time-Life Books, 1976.

Chapter 3

Bliss, E. L., and Branch, C. H. H. *Anorexia Nervosa*. New York: Paul B. Hoeber, Inc., 1960.

Bourne, P. E. (ed.). *Addiction*. New York, San Francisco, London: Academic Press, 1974.

Brown, B. B. *New Mind, New Body; Bio-feedback: New Directions for the Mind*. New York: Harper & Row, 1974.

Dillard, A. *Pilgrim at Tinker Creek*. New York: William Morrow, 1975.

Dudley, D. L., Verhey, J. W., Masuda, M., Martin, C. J., and Holmes, T. H. "Long term adjustment, prognosis, and death in irreversible diffuse obstructive pulmonary syndromes." *Psychosomatic Medicine* 31:310–25, 1969.

Engel, G. L. *Psychological Development in Health and Disease*. Philadelphia and London: W. B. Saunders Company, 1962.

Graham, D. T. Health, disease, and the mind-body problem: linguistic parallelism. *Psychosomatic Medicine* 29:52–71, 1967.

Kimball, C. P. "A predictive study of adjustment to cardiac surgery." *Journal of Thoracic and Cardiovascular Surgery* 58:891–96, 1969.

Weizenbaum, J. *Computer Power and Human Reason*. San Francisco: W. H. Freeman, 1976.

Chapter 4

Alderson, M. "Relationship between month of birth and month of death in the elderly." *British Journal of Preventative Social Medicine* 29:151–56, 1975.

Cannon, W. B. "Voodoo death." *Psychosomatic Medicine* 19:182–90, 1957.

Engel, G. L. "A life setting conducive to illness. The giving up given up complex." *Annals of Internal Medicine* 69:293–300, 1968.

"Happy death day." Editorial, *British Medical Journal* 12:423, 1975.

Hinkle, L. E., Jr., Christenson, W. N., Kane, F. D., Ostfeld, A., Thetford, W. N., and Wolff, H. G. "An investigation of the relation between life experience, personality characteristics, and general susceptibility to illness." *Psychosomatic Medicine* 20:278–95, 1958.

———, Pinsky, R. H., Bross, I. D. J., and Plummer, N. "The distribution of sickness disability in a homogeneous group of 'healthy adult men.'" *American Journal of Hygiene* 64:220–42, 1956.

———, Redmont, R., Plummer, N., and Wolff, H. G. "An examination of the relation between symptoms, disability, and serious illness in two homogeneous groups of men and women." *American Journal of Public Health* 50:1327–66, 1960.

Holmes, T. H., Goodell, H., Wolf, S., and Wolff, H. G. *The Nose, An Experimental Study of Reactions Within the Nose in Human Subjects During Varying Life Experiences*. Springfield, Ill.: Charles C Thomas, 1950.

Levy, N. B., editor. *Living or Dying, Adaptation to Hemodialysis*. Springfield, Ill.: Charles C Thomas, 1974.

Richter, C. P. "On the phenomenon of sudden death in animals and man." *Psychosomatic Medicine* 19:191–98, 1957.

Seligman, M. E. P. *Helplessness*. San Francisco: W. H. Freeman, 1975.

Stevenson, I. "Physical symptoms occurring with pleasurable emotional states." *American Journal of Psychiatry* 127:175–79, 1970.

Thomas, L. *The Lives of a Cell*. New York: Viking, 1974.

Wolff, H. G., Wolf, S., Grace, W. J., Holmes, T. H., Stevenson, I., Straub, L., Goodell, H., and Seton, P. "Changes in form and function of mucous membranes occurring as part of protective reaction patterns in man during period of life stress and emotional conflict." *Transactions of the Association of American Physicians* 61:313–34, 1948.

Chapter 5

Bramwell, S. T., Masuda, M., Wagner, N. N., and Holmes, T. H. "Psychosocial factors in athletic injuries: development and application of the Social and Athletic Readjustment Rating Scale (SARRS)." *Journal of Human Stress* 1:6–20, 1975.

Coddington, R. D. "The significance of life events as etiologic factors in the diseases of children. I. A survey of professional workers." *Journal of Psychosomatic Research* 16:7–18, 1972.

——. "The significance of life events as etiologic factors in the diseases of children. II. A study of a normal population." *Journal of Psychosomatic Research* 16:205–13, 1972.

Dohrenwend, B. S., and Dohrenwend, B. P. *Stressful Life Events, Their Nature and Effects.* New York: John Wiley & Sons, 1974.

Dudley, D. L., Roszell, D. K., Mules, J. E., and Hague, W. "Heroin vs. alcohol addiction: quantifiable psychosocial similarities and differences." *Journal of Psychosomatic Research* 18:327–35, 1974.

Gunderson, E. E. K., and Rahe, R. H. *Life Stress and Illness.* Springfield, Ill.: Charles C Thomas, 1974.

Harmon, D. K., Masuda, M., and Holmes, T. H. "The Social Readjustment Rating Scale: a cross-cultural study of Western Europeans and Americans." *Journal of Psychosomatic Research* 14: 391–400, 1970.

Hawkins, N. G., Davies, R., and Holmes, T. H. Evidence of psychosocial factors in the development of pulmonary tuberculosis. *American Review of Tuberculosis and Pulmonary Diseases* 75: 768–80, 1957.

Holmes, T. H., Hawkins, N. G., Bowerman, C. E., Clarke, E. R., and Joffe, J. R. "Psychosocial and psychophysiologic studies of tuberculosis." *Psychosomatic Medicine* 19:134–43, 1957.

———, and Masuda, M. Life change and illness susceptibility. In *Symposium on Separation and Depression*. J. P. Scott and E. C. Senay (eds.). Washington, D.C.: American Association for the Advancement of Science, Publication No. 94, 1973. Pp. 161–86.

———. "Psychosomatic syndrome: When mothers-in-law or other disasters visit, a person can develop a bad, bad cold or worse." *Psychology Today,* April 1972. Pp. 71–72 and 106.

Holmes, T. S., and Holmes, T. H. "Short-term intrusions into the life style routine." *Journal of Psychosomatic Research* 14:121–32, 1970.

Kissen, D. M. "Some psychosocial aspects of pulmonary tuberculosis." *International Journal of Social Psychiatry* 3:252–59, 1958.

Komaroff, A. L., Masuda, M., and Holmes, T. H. "The Social Readjustment Rating Scale: a comparative study of Negro, Mexican, and white Americans." *Journal of Psychosomatic Research* 12: 121–28, 1968.

Masuda, M., and Holmes, T. H. "Magnitude estimations of social readjustments." *Journal of Psychosomatic Research* 11:219–25, 1967.

———. "The Social Readjustment Rating Scale: a cross-cultural study of Japanese and Americans." *Journal of Psychosomatic Research* 11:227–37, 1967.

Rahe, R. H. "Multi-cultural correlations of life change scaling: America, Japan, Denmark and Sweden." *Journal of Psychosomatic Research* 13:191–95, 1969.

———, McKean, J. D., Jr., and Arthur, R. J. "A longitudinal study of life-change and illness patterns." *Journal of Psychosomatic Research* 10:355–66, 1967.

———, and Arthur, R. J. "Life-change patterns surrounding illness experience." *Journal of Psychosomatic Research* 11:341–45, 1968.

Sparer, P. J. (ed.). *Personality Stress and Tuberculosis.* New York: International University Press, 1956.

Toffler, A. *Future Shock*. New York: Random House, 1970.

Williams, C. C., Williams, R. A., Griswold, M. J., and Holmes, T. H. "Pregnancy and life change." *Journal of Psychosomatic Research* 19:123–29, 1975.

Woon, T., Masuda, M., Wagner, N. N., and Holmes, T. H. "The Social Readjustment Rating Scale: a cross-cultural study of Malaysians and Americans." *Journal of Cross-Cultural Psychology* 2:373–86, 1971.

Wyler, A. R., Masuda, M., and Holmes, T. H. "The Seriousness of Illness Rating Scale: reproducibility." *Journal of Psychosomatic Research* 14:59–64, 1970.

———. "Magnitude of life events and seriousness of illness." *Psychosomatic Medicine* 33:115–22, 1971.

Chapter 6

Berle, B. B., Pinsky, R. H., Wolf, S., and Wolff, H. G. "A clinical guide to prognosis in stress diseases." *Journal of the American Medical Association* 149:1624–28, 1952.

De Araujo, G., Dudley, D. L., and VanArsdel, P. P., Jr. "Psychosocial assets and severity of chronic asthma." *Journal of Allergy and Clinical Immunology* 50:257–63, 1972.

———, VanArsdel, P. P., Jr., Holmes, T. H., and Dudley, D. L. "Life change, coping ability and chronic intrinsic asthma." *Journal of Psychosomatic Research* 17:359–63, 1973.

Dudley, D. L., Verhey, J. W., Masuda, M., Martin, C. J., and Holmes, T. H. "Long-term adjustment, prognosis, and death in irreversible diffuse obstructive pulmonary syndromes." *Psychosomatic Medicine* 31:310–25, 1969.

Friedman, M., and Rosenman, R. H. *Type A Behavior and Your Heart*. New York: Knopf, 1974.

Grace, W. J., and Graham, D. T. "Relationship of specific attitudes and emotions to certain bodily diseases. *Psychosomatic Medicine* 14:243–51, 1952.

Graham, D. T., Lundy, R. M., Benjamin, L. S., Kabler, J. D., Lewis, W. C., Kunish, N. O., and Graham, F. K. "Specific attitudes in initial interviews with patients having different 'psychosomatic' diseases." *Psychosomatic Medicine* 24:257–66, 1962.

———, Stern, J. A., and Winokur, G. "Experimental investigation of the specificity of attitude hypothesis in psychosomatic disease." *Psychosomatic Medicine* 20:446–57, 1958.

Holmes, T. H., Joffe, J. R., Ketcham, J. W., and Sheehy, T. F. "Experimental study of prognosis." *Journal of Psychosomatic Research* 5:235–52, 1961.

Marmot, M. G. "Acculturation and coronary heart disease in Japanese-Americans." University of California, Berkeley School of Public Health. Unpublished data as of October 1976.

Stern, J. A., Winokur, G., Graham, D. T., and Graham, F. K. "Alterations in physiological measures during experimentally induced attitudes." *Journal of Psychosomatic Research* 5:73–82, 1961.

"This Question of Coping." Parts 1 through 11. Roche Laboratories. Hamburg, D. A. Consultant to Coping Series. 1974.

Chapters 7 and 8

Adler, R., MacRitchie, K., and Engel, G. L. "Psychologic processes and ischemic stroke." *Psychosomatic Medicine* 33:1–29, 1971. (Identical data on females as yet unpublished.)

Adsett, C. A., Schottstaedt, W. W., and Wolff, H. G. "Changes in coronary blood flow and other hemodynamic indicators induced by stressful interviews." *Psychosomatic Medicine* 24:331–36, 1962.

Amkraut, A., and Solomon, G. F. "From the symbolic stimulus to the pathophysiologic response: immune mechanisms." *International Journal of Psychiatry in Medicine* 5:541–63, 1974.

Backus, F. I., and Dudley, D. L. "Observations of psychosocial factors and their relationship to organic disease." *International Journal of Psychiatry in Medicine* 5:499–515, 1974.

Bahnson, C. B., Conference Chairman and Consulting Editor. Second Conference on Psychophysiological Aspects of Cancer. *Annals of the New York Academy of Sciences* 164:307–634, 1969.

Benson, H. *The Relaxation Response.* New York: William Morrow, 1975.

Brolley, M., Hollender, M. H. "Psychological problems of patients with myasthenia gravis." *Journal of Nervous and Mental Disease* 122:178–84, 1955.

Brown, C. C. "The parotid puzzle: a review of the literature on human salivation and its applications to psychophysiology." *Psychophysiology* 7:66–85, 1970.

Brown, W. A., and Mueller, P. S. "Psychological function in individuals with myotrophic lateral sclerosis." *Psychosomatic Medicine* 32:141–52, 1970.

Bruch, H. *Eating Disorders*. New York: Basic Books, Inc., 1973.

Chambers, W. N., and Reiser, M. F. "Emotional stress in the precipitation of congestive heart failure." *Psychosomatic Medicine* 15: 38–60, 1953.

Cobb, S., Schull, W. J., Harburg, E., and Kasl, S. V. "The Intrafamial transmission of rheumatoid arthritis: I–VIII." *Journal of Chronic Disease* 22:193–295, 1969.

Dekker, E., Pelser, H. E., Groen, J. "Conditioning as a cause of asthmatic attacks." *Journal of Psychosomatic Research* 2:97–108, 1957.

Dudley, D. L. In collaboration with Martin, C. J., Masuda, M., Ripley, H. S., and Holmes, T. H. *The Psychophysiology of Respiration in Health and Disease*. New York: Appleton-Century-Crofts, 1969. P. 342.

Dukes, H. T., and Vieth, R. G. "Cerebral arteriography during migraine prodrome and headache." *Neurology* 14:436–39, 1964.

Duncan, C. H., Stevenson, I. P., and Ripley, H. S. "Life situations, emotions, and paroxysmal auricular arrhythmias." *Psychosomatic Medicine* 12:23–37, 1950.

Engel, G. L. *Fainting* (2nd ed.). Springfield, Ill.: Charles C Thomas, 1962.

Fieve, R. R. *Mood Swings*. New York: Bantam, 1975.

Fischer, H. K., Dlin, B. M., Winters, W. L., Jr., Hagner, S. B., Russell, G. W., and Weiss, E. Emotional factors in coronary occlusion. II. Time patterns and factors related to onset. *Psychosomatics* 5:280–91, 1964.

Friedman, M., Roseman, R. H. "Association of specific overt behavior pattern with blood and cardiovascular findings: blood clotting time, incidence of arcus senilis and clinical artery disease." *Journal of the American Medical Association* 169:1286–296, 1959.

———, Roseman, R. H., and Carroll, V. "Changes in the serum cholesterol and blood clotting time in men subjected to cyclic variation of occupational stress." *Circulation* 17:852–61, 1958.

Grace, W. J., Seton, P. H., Wolf, S., and Wolff, H. G. "Studies of the human colon: I. Variations in concentration of lysozyme with life situation and emotional state." *American Journal of Medical Science* 217:241–51, 1949.

——, Wolf, S., and Wolff, H. G. "Life situations, emotions and chronic ulcerative colitis." *Journal of the American Medical Association* 142:1044–48, 1950.

Graham, D. T. "Cutaneous vascular reactions in Raynaud's disease and in states of hostility, anxiety, and depression." *Psychosomatic Medicine* 17:200–7, 1955.

——. "The relation of psoriasis to attitude and to vascular reactions of the human skin." *Journal of Investigative Dermatology* 22: 379–88, 1954.

——. "The pathogenesis of hives: experimental study of life situations, emotions, and cutaneous vascular reactions." *Research Publications Association for Research in Nervous and Mental Disease* 29:987–1009, 1950.

——, Kabler, J. D., and Lunsford, L. "Vasovagal fainting: a diphasic response." *Psychosomatic Medicine* 23:493–507, 1961.

——, and Wolf, S. "The relation of eczema to attitude and to vascular reactions of the human skin." *Journal of Laboratory and Clinical Medicine* 42:238–54, 1953.

Greene, W. A., Jr. "Psychological factors and reticuloendothelial disease. I. Preliminary observations on a group of males with lymphomas and leukemias." *Psychosomatic Medicine* 16:220–30, 1954.

——, and Miller, G. "Psychological factors and reticuloendothelial disease. IV. Observations on a group of children and adolescents with leukemia: an interpretation of disease development in terms of the mother-child unit." *Psychosomatic Medicine* 20:124–44, 1958.

——, Young, L. E., and Swisher, S. N. "Psychological factors and reticuloendothelial disease. II. Observations on a group of women with lymphomas and leukemias." *Psychosomatic Medicine* 18: 234–303, 1956.

Harburg, E., Erfurt, J. C., Hauenstein, L. S., et al.: "Socio-ecological stress, suppressed hostility, skin color, and black-white male blood pressure: Detroit." *Psychosomatic Medicine* 35:276–96, 1973.

Hawkins, N. G., Davies, R., and Holmes, T. H. "Evidence of psychosocial factors in the development of pulmonary tuberculosis." *American Review of Tuberculosis and Pulmonary Disease* 75: 768–80, 1957.

Heisel, J. S. "Life changes as etiologic factors in juvenile rheumatoid arthritis." *Journal of Psychosomatic Research* 17:411–20, 1972.

Heninger, G. R., and Mueller, P. S. "Carbohydrate metabolism in mania." *Archives of General Psychiatry* 23:310–18, 1970.

Henry, J. P., Stephens, P. M., and Watson, F. M. C. "Force breeding, social disorder and mammary tumor formation in CBA/USC mouse colonies." *Psychosomatic Medicine* 27:277–83, 1975.

Hinkle, L. E., Jr., and Wolf, S. "Experimental study of life situations, emotions, and the occurrence of acidosis in a juvenile diabetic." *American Journal of Medical Sciences* 217:130–35, 1949.

———, Conger, G. B., and Wolf, S. "Studies on diabetes mellitus: the relation of stressful life situations to the concentration of ketone bodies in the blood of diabetic and non-diabetic humans." *Journal of Clinical Investigation* 29:754–69, 1950.

———, and Wolf, S. "Studies in diabetes mellitus: changes in glucose, ketone, and water metabolism during stress." *Research Publications Association for Research in Nervous and Mental Disease* 29:338–89, 1950.

———. "Importance of life stress in course and management of diabetes mellitus. *Journal of the American Medical Association* 148: 513–20, 1952.

———. "A summary of experimental evidence relating life stress to diabetes mellitus." *Journal of the Mount Sinai Hospital* 19:537–70, 1952.

Holmes, T. H. "Infectious diseases and human ecology." *Journal of the Indian Medical Profession* 10:4825–29, 1964.

———. "Psychosocial and psychophysiological studies of tuberculosis." In *Physiological Correlates of Psychological Disorders*. Roessler, R., and Greenfield, N. S. (eds.). Madison: University of Wisconsin Press, 1962. Pp. 239–55.

———, and Wolff, H. G. "Life situations, emotions and backache." *Research Publications Association for Research in Nervous and Mental Disease* 29:750–72, 1950.

——, Treuting, T., and Wolff, H. G. "Life situations, emotions and nasal disease: evidence on summative effects exhibited in patients with 'hay fever.'" *Psychosomatic Medicine* 25:403–19, 1963.

Hong, M. K., and Holmes, T. H. "Transient diabetes mellitus associated with culture change." *Archives of General Psychiatry* 29: 683–87, 1973.

Kehoe, M., and Ironside, W. "Studies on the experimental evocation of depressive responses using hypnosis: II. The influence of depressive responses upon the secretion of gastric acid." *Psychosomatic Medicine* 25:403–19, 1963.

Kiely, W. F. "From the symbolic stimulus to the pathophysiologic response: neurophysiological mechanisms." *International Journal of Psychiatry in Medicine* 5:517–29, 1974.

Kissen, D. M. "The significance of personality in lung cancer in men." *Annals of the New York Academy of Science* 125:820–26, 1966.

Lipowski, Z. J. "Psychophysiological cardiovascular disorders." In *Comprehensive Textbook of Psychiatry*. Freedman, A. M., Kaplan, H. I., and Sadock, B. J. (eds.). Baltimore: Williams and Wilkins, 1974.

Lium, R. "Etiology of ulcerative colitis." *Archives of Internal Medicine* 63:210–25, 1939.

Marcussen, R. M., and Wolff, H. G. "A formulation of the dynamics of the migraine attack." *Psychosomatic Medicine* 11:251–56, 1949.

Masuda, M., Notske, R. N., and Holmes, T. H. "Catecholamine excretion and asthmatic behavior." *Journal of Psychosomatic Research* 10:255–62, 1966.

Mathe, A. A., and Knapp, P. H. "Emotional and adrenal reactions to stress in bronchial asthma." *Psychosomatic Medicine* 33:323–40, 1971.

Mei-Tal, V., Meyerowitz, S., and Engel, G. L. "The role of psychological process in a somatic disorder: multiple sclerosis." *Psychosomatic Medicine* 32:67–86, 1970.

Meyer, K., Gellhorn, A., Prudden, J. F., et al. "Lysozyme activity in ulcerative alimentary disease: II." *American Journal of Medicine* 5:496–502, 1948.

Mittelmann, B., and Wolff, H. G. "Emotions and gastroduodenal function: experimental studies on patients with gastritis, duodenitis, and peptic ulcer." *Psychosomatic Medicine* 4:5–61, 1942.

Morris, H. G., DeRoche, G., and Earle, M. R. "Urinary excretion of epinephrine and norepinephrine in asthmatic children." *Journal of Allergy and Clinical Immunology* 50:138–45, 1972.

O'Brien, M. D. "The relationship between aura symptoms and cerebral blood flow changes in the prodrome of migraine." *Proceedings of the International Headache Symposium,* May 16–18, 1971. Delessio, D. J., Dalsgaard-Nielsen, T., and Diamond, S. (eds.). Elsinore, Denmark; Basel, Switzerland: Sandoz, 1971.

Rahe, R. H., Meyer, M., Smith, M., Kjaer, G., and Holmes, T. H. "Social stress and illness onset." *Journal of Psychosomatic Research* 8:35–44, 1964.

———, and Holmes, T. H. "Social, psychologic and psychophysiologic aspects of inguinal hernia." *Journal of Psychosomatic Research* 8:487–91, 1965.

Rappaport, M., Hopkins, H. K., and Hall, K. "Auditory signal detection in paranoid and nonparanoid schizophrenics." *Archives of General Psychiatry* 27:747–52, 1972.

Rosen, H., and Lidz, T. "Emotional factors in the precipitation of recurrent diabetic acidosis." *Psychosomatic Medicine* 11:211–15, 1949.

Schneider, R. A., and Zangari, V. M. "Variations in clotting time, relative viscosity, and other physiochemical properties of the blood accompanying physical and emotional stress in the normotensive and hypertensive subject." *Psychosomatic Medicine* 13: 289–303, 1951.

Schottstaedt, W. W., Grace, W. J., and Wolff, H. G. "Life situations, behavior, attitudes, emotions, and renal excretion of fluid and electrolytes, I, II, III, IV." *Journal of Psychosomatic Research* 1:75–83, 147–59, 177–85, 203–11, and 287–98, 1956.

Simons, D. J., Day, E., Goodell, H., and Wolff, H. G. "Experimental studies on headache: muscles of the scalp and neck as sources of pain." *Research Publications Association for Research in Nervous and Mental Disease* 23:228–44, 1943.

Stein, S. P., and Charles, E. "Emotional factors in juvenile diabetes mellitus: a study of early life experience of adolescent diabetics." *American Journal of Psychiatry* 128:700–4, 1971.

Stern, J. A., Winokur, G., Graham, D. T., and Graham, F. K. "Alterations in physiological measures during experimentally induced attitudes." *Journal of Psychosomatic Research* 5:73–82, 1961.

Stevenson, I. P., and Duncan, C. H. "Alterations in cardiac function and circulatory efficiency during periods of life stress as shown by changes in the rate, rhythm, electrocardiograph pattern and output of the heart in those with cardiovascular disease." *Research Publications Association for Research in Nervous and Mental Disease* 29:799–817, 1950.

——, and Wolff, H. G. "Life situations, emotions and bronchial mucus." *Psychosomatic Medicine* 11:223–27, 1949.

Van der Velde, C. D., and Gordon, M. W. "Manic depressive illness, diabetes mellitus and lithium carbonate." *Archives of General Psychiatry* 21:278–485, 1969.

Weiner, H. (ed.). *Advances in Psychosomatic Medicine,* Vol. 6: *Duodenal Ulcer.* Basel: Karger, 1971.

Weiss, E., Dlin, B., Rollin, H. R., Fischer, H. K., and Bepler, C. R. "Emotional factors in coronary occlusion." *Archives of Internal Medicine* 99:628–41, 1957.

Wolf, S., Cardon, P. V., Jr., Shepard, E. M., and Wolff, H. G. *Life Stress and Essential Hypertension.* Baltimore: Williams and Wilkins, 1955.

——, Pfeiffer, J. B., Ripley, H. S., Winter, O. S., and Wolff, H. G. "Hypertension as a reaction pattern to stress; summary of experimental data on variations in blood pressure and renal blood flow." *Annals of Internal Medicine* 29:1056–79, 1948.

Wolff, H. G., Lorenz, T. H., and Graham, D. T. "Stress, emotions and human sebum: their relevance to acne vulgaris." *Transactions of the Association of American Physicians* 64:435–44, 1951.

——. *Headache and Other Head Pain* (2nd ed.). New York: Oxford University Press, 1963.

——. "Life stress and cardiovascular disorders." *Circulation* 1:187–203, 1950.

Chapter 9

Birk, L. *Biofeedback: Behavioral Medicine.* New York and London: Grune and Stratton, 1973.

Bonica, J. (ed.). *Advances in Neurology Volume 4: Pain.* New York: Raven Press, 1974.

Crue, B. L. (ed.). *Pain.* New York: Academic Press, 1975.

Dudley, D. L., Holmes, T. H., Martin, C. J., and Ripley, H. S. "Hypnotically induced facsimile of pain." *Archives of General Psychiatry* 15:198–204, 1966.

——, Martin, C. J., and Holmes, T. H. "Dyspnea: Psychologic and physiologic observations." *Journal of Psychosomatic Research* 11:325–39, 1968.

Febrega, H. *Disease and Social Behavior.* Cambridge, Mass., and London: The MIT Press, 1974.

Greenfield, N. S., and Sternbach, R. A. (eds.). *Handbook of Psychophysiology.* New York: Holt, Rinehart & Winston, Inc., 1972.

Holmes, T. H., and Dudley, D. L. *Comfort-Productivity Scale.* Copyright, 1974. Published by: Washington Thoracic Society, Medical Section of the Washington Lung Association, 1974.

Manry, R. *Tinkerbelle.* New York: Harper & Row, 1965.

Musaph, H. (ed.). *Mechanisms of Symptom Formation.* Basel, Switzerland: S. Karger, 1974.

Siegel, R. K., and West, L. J. *Hallucinations.* New York: John Wiley and Sons, 1975.

Silverman, S. *Psychological Aspects of Physical Symptoms.* New York: Appleton-Century-Crofts, 1968.

Wolff, H. G., and Wolf, S. *Pain.* Springfield, Ill.: Charles C Thomas, 1958.

Chapter 10

Backus, F. I., and Dudley, D. L. "Observations of psychosocial factors and their relationship to organic disease." *International Journal of Psychiatry in Medicine* 5:499–515, 1974.

Graham, D. T. "Cutaneous vascular reactions in Raynaud's disease and in states of hostility, anxiety, and depression." *Psychosomatic Medicine* 17:200–7, 1955.

———. "The pathogenesis of hives: experimental study of life situations, emotions, and cutaneous vascular reactions." *Research Publications Association for Research in Nervous and Mental Disease* 29:987–1009, 1950.

———, Lundy, R. M., Benjamin, L. S., et al. "Specific attitudes in initial interviews with patients having different 'psychosomatic' diseases." *Psychosomatic Medicine* 24:257–66, 1962.

Mittelmann, B., and Wolff, H. G. "Affective states and skin temperature: experimental study of subjects with 'cold hands' and Raynaud's syndrome." *Psychosomatic Medicine* 1:271–92, 1939.

———, and Wolff, H. G. "Emotions and skin temperature: observations on patients during psychotherapeutic interviews." *Psychosomatic Medicine* 5:211–31, 1943.

Porter, K. A. *Ship of Fools*. Boston: Little, Brown, 1962.

Chapter 11

Burnam, T. *The Dictionary of Misinformation*. New York: Thomas Y. Crowell, 1975.

Craighead, F. C., Jr., and Craighead, J. J. *How to Survive on Land and Sea*. Annapolis: United States Naval Institute, 1943.

Leaf, A. *Youth in Old Age*. New York: McGraw-Hill, 1975.

Metcalf, G. R. *Up from Within*. New York: Random House, 1970.

Snyder, S. H. *The Troubled Mind: A Guide to Release from Distress*. New York: McGraw-Hill, 1976.